a sense of place

Barbara Hume, Frances James and Ann Kerr

Line drawings by Kathie Barrs

First Published in 1995 by
BELAIR PUBLICATIONS LIMITED
P.O. Box 12, Twickenham, England, TW1 2QL

© 1995 Barbara Hume, Frances James and Ann Kerr
Series Editor Robyn Gordon
Designed by Richard Souper
Photography by Kelvin Freeman
Typesetting by Belair
Printed in Hong Kong through World Print Ltd
ISBN 0 947882 53 7

Acknowledgements

The Authors and Publishers would like to thank the following for their support and contributions during the preparation of this book:

Sophie Allen for wall displays; Daisy John, Nicholas Thomas, Abigail Davidson, Carol McCarthy and Matthew Kerr; Helen Gwynne for the pond collage on page 57; the children of East Sheen Primary School, London, SWl5; Jane Lee for the batik display below; Kate Thorp and Elizabeth Crowe for the loan of Peruvian artefacts and photographs; and Heather Hacking and Hannah Souper for the cover artwork.

Batik pictures inspired by St. Lucia (see instructions on page 72)

Contents

Introduction

Geographical Skills and the Home Area

Beginnings   5
The local area: a sense of place   7
Local Amenities   9
Geographical language   10
Using photographs   12
The language of position   13
Journeys - planning a route   17
Maps and map-making   19

Topics

Buildings   25
    Dwellings   26
    Shops   28
    Factories   31
Work and leisure   33
    Leisure   33
    Work   36
Transport   39
Food and farming   45
Water   52
Weather   58
    Weather forecasting 59
    Wind   60
    Rain   63
    Sun   63
Seasons   64

**Comparison of the home area
with another locality**   67

**Comparison of the home area
with a locality overseas - Peru**   69

Introduction

- In presenting *A Sense of Place,* the authors aim to provide teachers with ideas for developing children's geographical knowledge, skills and understanding, and awareness of their own environment and contrasting localities.

- Activities are based, wherever possible, on direct, first-hand experience, focusing initially on the immediate locality of the school, and going on to explore contrasting localities at home and overseas.

- The first section of the book takes a look at the local community, investigating services and amenities, landmarks and geographical features, and suggests activities that will encourage children to develop a critical awareness of their own environment. There are ideas for introducing geographical language, and for using visits, fieldwork and photographs to develop a sense of place in young children.

- The book provides suggestions for activities to develop map skills, introducing children to the concepts of location and direction, scale, perspective and distance, and the use of conventional symbols.

- A series of geographical topics including buildings, work and leisure, transport, food and farming, water and weather, allow for further in-depth study of the local area related to a theme.

- The final sections of the book offer practical suggestions for developing comparative studies of the immediate area of the school with other localities at home and overseas.

- Throughout the book we emphasise the importance of children being involved in practical activity, increasing their understanding and knowledge of places and geographical themes by carrying out research, making observations and comparisons, by making personal responses to their own environment and recording those responses in a creative and exciting way.

Barbara Hume, Frances James
and Ann Kerr

Beginnings

Sitting in Richmond Park ....

SIMILARITIES AND DIFFERENCES
Discussion

Talk to the children about how we are different. Compare physical characteristics such as facial features, colour of eyes, skin, and hair; height, weight and other body measurements such as length of reach, circumference of head, handspan and length of fingers. Talk about other things that make us different: likes and dislikes (food, television programmes, activities); opinions; jobs; the languages spoken; religions and beliefs; types of housing; size of family; aspects of family history. Talk about similarities that are shared - the basic needs of life such as food, warmth, shelter, love, education. Promote community awareness in young children by talking about the shared activities: going to school together, living in the same area, using the same shops, enjoying clubs, parks and play areas, watching the same television programmes, sharing local forms of transport, and services in the community such as the doctor and dentist.

Activities

- 'Where in the world am I?' Play the popular game of writing the fullest address possible:
  John Anderson
  7 Park Road
  Bradstock
  Surrey
  England
  United Kingdom
  Europe
  The World
  The Universe.

- Make an address spiral as shown in the diagram. Starting from a picture or photograph placed in the middle, the child writes the address around the drawn spiral shape. These are then cut out and hung on low strings to display.

- Make 'identikit' pictures. These can take the form of WANTED posters, with the children describing themselves or a friend.
- **Paint self-portraits.** Portraits of famous people in the past often included 'clues' about their lifestyle and their interests. Ask the children to include indicators such as special toys, clothes or artefacts in their pictures.

My self portrait: Can you guess what I like doing?

- Make individual passports including a photograph or picture and personal details such as name, national status, occupation, date and place of birth, place of residence, height and distinguishing marks. These can be used in role play involving travel and journeys.
- Make a 'Guess Who?' display for parents and other children. Make and cut out shadow profiles from black paper using a projector, and display these together with personal details about the character, for example, 'I have two brothers and I live in a flat. I have a dog, and I like playing tennis. Who am I?'
- Create a class data file. Ask children to decide upon the information to include, for example, height, weight, colour of eyes, hair, number in family, type of dwelling, etc. Construct graphs and pie charts using the computer.
- Write narrative stories which include as many personal details as possible, such as where the characters live, how they travel, and aspects of their family life. Ask children to write their own personal 'A day in the life of ....' stories. Illustrate the stories and include times of the day. These can be used later to make comparisons with the experiences of children living in other areas of the country, or other parts of the world.

The local area: a sense of place

Talk to the children about their favourite places in the local area. Ask where they would take visitors. Are there any famous sites or places of interest nearby?

● Write poems inspired by a locality and display with paintings and photographs. Ask children to write notes 'in situ' to be later crafted into the finished work. (See photograph above.)

● Make a collection of postcards, photographs, and brochures featuring places of special interest in the area. Display these around a local map and match the pictures to their location. Ask the children to write about visits they have made, and to explain why the place attracts visitors.

● Collect pictures of artists' representations of areas of special interest or landmarks, either in your local area or in your general area of the country. For example, look at paintings of views, bridges, buildings, mountains, lakes, and coastlines and see how they differ. Do they show different weather conditions, different times of the year, or different times of the day? Compare pictures and paintings with photographs of the same landscape.

● Choose a favourite place locally (urban or rural) and select different media to create pictures or paintings. Encourage children to choose a medium, tools and materials to suit the landscape. For example, card or block printing may be suitable for producing the hard edges and straight lines required by a cityscape. Talk to the children about perspective, foreground, middle ground and background. Draw the children's attention to the horizon of the landscape or cityscape. Talk about 'where the land meets the sky', or 'as far as the eye can see'. Discuss how their pictures can reflect the mood of a place, whether it is a peaceful rural scene or a busy townscape.

● As a long term project, build up a collection of photographs of one particular place in the local environment taken at different times of the year, and in different weather conditions. These can be displayed in an album, with a commentary written by the children, for example, 'A year in the life of our pond and wildlife garden'.

● Talk about how the mood of a place can differ. Ask the children to suggest adjectives: places can be noisy, quiet, busy, interesting, solemn, exciting, deserted, beautiful, dangerous, comfortable, or perhaps 'creepy'. Ask the children to choose places in the local area, to describe and draw them.

Environmental studies

Encourage a critical awareness of the local environment by discussing the things that children like and dislike about the area in which they live. Start with a brainstorming session. Ask 'What is good about our environment? What is bad?' Draw up a list of likes and dislikes. Consider any recent or proposed changes. What effect will these have on the area?

● Ask children to draw a map or picture of the local area on a prepared worksheet (see line drawing) to list significant problems (dog fouling, traffic noise and fumes, aircraft noise, litter, graffiti, pollution of water, etc.) and where they are found.

Our local area.

Problem	Where
dog fouling	alleyways
litter	park
graffiti	walls
traffic noise	cross road
fumes	high street

● After identifying any problems, talk about action (both large and small scale) that could be taken to improve the environment. For example, the children may decide to mount a poster campaign to raise awareness of issues such as a problem with litter in the school grounds, or they may choose to instigate a 'litter pick' themselves.

● For larger issues, the children could decide to write to the local papers enlisting the help of the readers, to members of the PTA or governing body, to their MP, or to the local councillors asking for the council to take specific action. They may want to form a mini action group or support a local pressure group. The children should be encouraged to research their chosen topic to determine responsibility so that the right people can be targeted. They should also be encouraged to make practical suggestions for what could be done. When outside agencies are contacted, teachers may need to include a covering letter explaining the context of the children's letters, their concerns, and the starting point for their project.

Local amenities

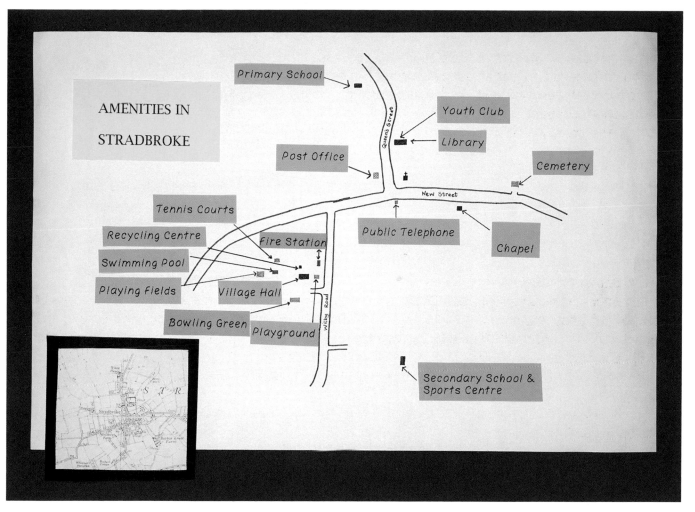

AMENITIES IN STRADBROKE

Primary School

Youth Club

Library

Post Office

Cemetery

Queens Street

New Street

Tennis Courts

Recycling Centre

Swimming Pool

Playing Fields

Fire Station

Public Telephone

Chapel

Village Hall

Bowling Green

Playground

Witby Road

Secondary School & Sports Centre

Preparation
Ask the children if they know about any clubs, societies or organisations that exist within the local area that provide leisure activities. Make a list of all the ones they know about. Ask the children to interview their parents or adults within the school about their leisure time. Either take the children to the local library, or collect from the library, all the available leaflets and information about local facilities.

Take the children on a walk in the local area. Organise them into small groups and ask each group to collect particular information, for example, opening times of any facilities, accessibility for the community, how to join a particular organisation, age range permitted, etc.

On return to school provide the children with a large map of the local area. Ask them to make labels of all the places they have found. Ask the children to place their labels on the map with a ribbon pointing to where it can be found. (See photograph above.)

Follow-up Activities
● Ask the children to design a piece of play equipment for the local playground.
● Ask the children to write to a local or national organisation requesting further information.
● Ask the children to interview their parents or other adults about what else they would like to have available locally.
● Make a display of posters, leaflets, notices about local facilities.
● Write to a school in a different part of the country to ask about the facilities in their area.
● Invite a speaker from a local organisation to talk to the children, for example, from Community Education, swimming pool, cinema, sports centre.

Geographical language

As with all subject specific language, it is important to introduce particular vocabulary clearly, and to accompany it with first-hand experience, whenever possible.

Some of the terms will already be in the children's vocabulary, but use and experience will refine the children's appreciation of the features. In many cases the terms are distinguished by degree or size - for example, the difference between a hill and a mountain. Young children find the appreciation of size and distance particularly challenging.

Settlements

● When introducing vocabulary, start from the children's existing knowledge. For example, if you want to teach the children the difference between a village, town and a city, start from the example in which the children live. Ask them to say where they live and whether they think it is a city, town or village. When the children have decided the category, ask them why they made that decision. Encourage them to think of other examples of settlements in the same category. Consider, with the children, if these places share the same features.

● Broaden the discussion to include the other categories of settlements. Again, draw on the children's knowledge and extend this with pictures of towns, cities and villages. Include aerial photographs to develop a sense of the size.
When the children have established a list of the features of the different settlements, divide the class into three groups. Tell them that they have to create an imaginary village, town and city. Provide large pieces of paper and a range of paints and collage materials. When they have finished their picture, ask them to think of a name for their settlement. The children complete pieces of writing describing their picture and the activities and features of the settlement. (See photograph on facing page.)

Making model landscapes

● Making models of features enhances the children's appreciation of features. Using papier mâché can take a very long time, but the time can be reduced by using chicken wire and padding out the elevations with crumpled up newspaper. Impress on the children that they have to be very careful when using wire.

Provide groups of children with large pieces of thick strong card. Tell them that you want them to make a landscape with a mountain, some hills, rivers and streams feeding the river. Show them how to use the wire and newspaper. When they have made the base, give them strips of newspaper and wallpaper paste. Then lay the pasted strips of paper over the model until the wire does not show through and there is a smooth surface. When the models are dry, the children can paint them.

Smallbury village

**Comparing cities and villages
(see Settlements on facing page)**

Bigbury city

This activity can be extended by asking some children to add settlements, facilities, communication systems, etc. When the children add them, ask them to justify their decisions - for example, why they have not put a town on the top of a mountain. Such questioning will develop in the children a more sophisticated idea of how geographical features affect our lives and the decisions that we make.

Visits

Many of the ideas in this book are supported by making visits to see certain features or geographical factors. Many of these visits can be made in the close vicinity of the school or even in the school grounds, and do not involve complicated transport arrangements. The benefits of such outings are increased by careful planning, involving the children.

Establish clear objectives for the trips. What do you want the children to see? How are you going to ensure that they truly appreciate what they see? How are the children going to record their observations? What equipment is necessary? What support materials (books, photographs, models) can you use? How will the visit be followed up when you return to class? Is it necessary for the whole class to go? Would it be possible to set the task for the children to complete on their way to school to encourage independent study?

Such preparations will maximise the learning opportunities for the children.

Using photographs

to introduce geographical language and to develop a sense of place

Compile a resource bank of photographs and pictures not only of specific areas to be studied but also images depicting a range of geographical features, weather conditions, landscapes, and peoples of the world engaged in a variety of activities. These can then be used to promote discussions relating to geographical themes. Try to build up an awareness that appearances can be deceptive. Talk about and compare impressions given by black and white images and colour photographs.

- Ask the children:
  'What time of the year do you think this is?'
  'What work do you think people do in this area?'
  'How do people travel from place to place?'
  'How do you think people spend their spare time?'
  Make comparisons with the children's own lifestyles.
- Ask the children to sort pictures according to different criteria:
  town or country (urban or rural)?
  home or abroad?
  hot or cold climate?
  high or low ground?
  Encourage the children to look for evidence to support their decisions.
- **Discuss what characters might be saying in the photographs and write speech bubbles for them.**

- Ask the children to engage in role play, acting out what they think is happening in the photograph. Ask them to make up details about individual characters using evidence extracted from the picture. The children could enact what they thought happened before and after, freeze-framing the moment that the photograph was taken.
- Encourage observational skills by asking a child to describe a picture while another draws it.
- Write captions for photographs.
- Extend the frame. Ask children to paint or draw what is happening beyond the view.

The language of position

Discussion

Introduce vocabulary such as near, far, distant, overseas, abroad, close, local, surroundings, vicinity, neighbourhood, district, and area. Talk about places and things ranging from the very near to the most distant. Produce definitions for each zone in discussion with the children - for example:

       near - in view, you can touch it

       quite near - within walking distance

       further away - requiring a journey by transport

       a long way - travelling abroad/overseas

       very far away - the other side of the world

       very, very far away - outer space

Prepare worksheets (size A3) as shown in the photograph above. Ask children to draw and label places and things in the appropriate zones.

● Research phrases and sayings meaning near and far. Draw up a list and ask children to illustrate some of them.

Near: a step away, within striking distance, a stone's throw away, within spitting distance, a hair's breadth, within earshot, on one's doorstep, in one's own backyard, under one's nose.

Far: at the world's end, to the back of beyond, over the horizon, as far as the eye can see, over the hills and far away, to the ends of the earth, light years away, far-flung.

● Promote 'global awareness' by instigating small research projects. Children can build up fact files, finding out from family, friends and neighbours where their clothes, household appliances and family cars are manufactured; where our food comes from; where penfriends or relatives live; where they have travelled to; or where famous athletes and sports stars come from. These places can then be located on world maps and globes. Food labels, postcards, flags, stamps, pictures and topical newspaper articles can be matched to maps for display.

Vocabulary relating to position and direction

Activities to introduce positional language such as up, down, on, under, over, above, below, next to, behind, in front of, left, right.

- Play a game 'I'm thinking of an object in this room'. The children have to guess the object by asking positional questions, for example: Is it near the door? Is it on a table?
- Carry out a treasure hunt where the teacher hides an object in the classroom and the children hunt for it, again by asking questions regarding its position.
- Play a game like 'Pin the Tail on a Donkey' in which one child is blindfolded and given directions to attach an item to a picture. Alternatively, one child can describe a picture while another draws it according to the directions. Play a 'behind the screen' game where one child describes a model made from Lego or building bricks, while the child on the other side of the screen builds the model, according to the instructions given.
- **Collect nursery rhymes and songs** that contain positional and directional language, for example, 'Incy Wincy Spider', 'The Grand Old Duke of York', 'Hickory Dickory Dock', 'Goosey Goosey, Gander'.

Poems and songs can be made into an anthology illustrated by the children.

- Make an illustrated class book called 'What goes up? What comes down?'
- Draw a picture of a bridge. Draw people, creatures and things that travel on and under the bridge.
- **Sort things that travel underground, on land, and in the air,** and record using the worksheet shown in the line drawing.

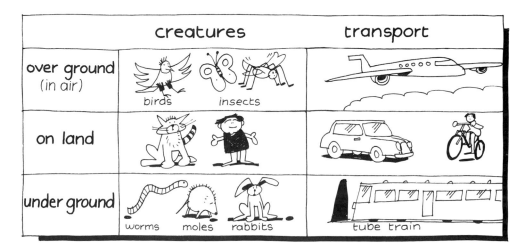

Draw what you can see directly in front of you. Draw a picture of what is behind you.

Make a lift-the-flap book illustrating a hide and seek story.

In gym and games, emphasise directions: 'side-step to the left'; 'stretch your right leg above your head'; 'pat a ball using alternate hands, saying left and right as you strike the ball'.

Ask the children in groups to design and draw an obstacle course using large and small apparatus. The finished plans should show the path to be taken using arrows and drawings of figures. The children could also record directions on a tape. The obstacle courses can then be constructed in the gym and enjoyed by everyone.

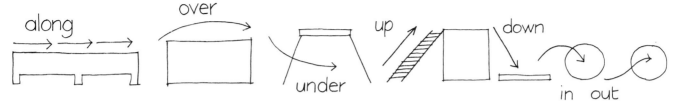

Read stories that contain a clear route and a range of directional language, for example, *Rosie's Walk, Bears in the Night, Going on a Bear Hunt. The Faber Book of Nursery Verse,* (ed. Barbara Ireson) contains a section entitled 'Walks, rides and journeys'.

Sing and play the 'Hokey Cokey' dance. Another rhyme featuring left and right is:

Here we go looby loo	Put your right hand in,
Here we go looby light,	Put your right hand out,
Here we go looby loo,	Shake it a little, a little,
All on a Saturday night.	And turn yourself about.

Make handprint pictures and patterns using two colours - one for the left hand and a contrasting colour for the right.

Make a graph to show who is left-handed and who is right-handed in the class. Ask the children to investigate the handedness of family members.

Activities using PIP (a programmable toy) and LOGO.

Set the children a series of challenges:

- Program PIP to travel forwards, backwards, to turn left and right.
- Send PIP to a partner.
- Make Pip turn all the way around - through 360°.
- Program PIP to turn in a clockwise direction, to turn in an anticlockwise direction.
- Introduce the vocabulary 'turning through 90°' in relation to right angled turns, and ask the children to make PIP carry out a right-angled turn to the left and to the right. Talk about one-quarter turns, half turns and three-quarter turns.
- Send PIP on short journeys to visit another room.
- Ask the children to construct a maze (or some kind of obstacle course) for PIP using large building blocks. Program PIP to travel through the maze.
- Make some large floor-mat games for PIP to travel across. Simple shapes such as a ladder, a rectangular grid or a space station are the most effective. (Older children can design mats for younger children as a design and technology challenge.)
- Similar games can be made for use with LOGO by attaching an OHP overlay to the computer screen.

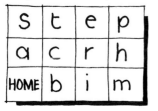

Program PIP to visit squares to collect letters to make words.

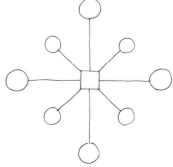

- Make a large floor map showing the points of the compass.
  Ask the children to make PIP travel to different points.

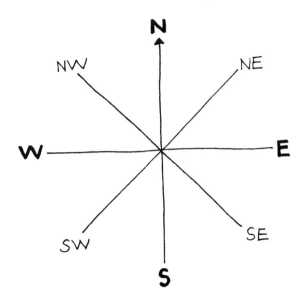

- Paint a large compass rose on the playground floor. Involve the children in deciding the best location for the compass rose.
- Find and mark north, south, east and west in different areas of the school, and in the school grounds at every opportunity.
- Play a game of 'Simon says...' in which the teacher or a child gives the children directions such as 'Simon says take five paces north and two paces east.'
- Relate the points of the compass to the position of the sun in the sky, and to the changing shadows.
- Older children will be able to investigate the differences between magnetic north, grid north, and the true/polar north.
- Demonstrate how to use a compass to find magnetic north. Show the children how to orientate a map so that the north arrow on the map points in the same direction as the compass needle.
- Look at a map of the local area and look for place names that include the words north, south, east and west. Observe their relative positions.
- Make a collection of poems and rhymes that feature the points of the compass.

> Mr East gave a feast
> Mr North laid the cloth
> Mr West did his best;
> Mr South burnt his mouth
> With eating a cold potato.

Journeys: planning a route

Our maps show how Fantastic Mr Fox reached the farms to get the food.

Discussion

Talk to the children about journeys they have made. Which was their longest journey, and how did they travel? Ask them why they used those particular forms of transport. Remind the children of previous shared journeys such as class outings and visits. Talk about short journeys that we make every day - to school, to the shops, to the park, to visit family and friends - and also short journeys that we make within the school itself.

● Ask each child to describe to a partner his/her journey to school. Encourage the children to use directional language (such as turn right, turn left, straight ahead, cross the road, go past) and to identify landmarks on their route as well as indicating with their hands (the natural thing to do!).

● Ask the children to draw their own route maps of their journey to school including important landmarks that they see on the way.

● Ask the children to trace the route from home to school on large scale maps of the local area. The children can then compare these maps with their own versions.

● Plan a journey within the school. Make a set of cards with places written or drawn on them. Split the cards into two piles and ask the children to choose a card from each pile. The first place is their starting point, the second place is their eventual destination within the school grounds.
  - Ask the children in pairs to write or tape directions describing their intended route to their destination.
  - The children then make their journey and amend their first draft if necessary, adding landmarks and more precise directions.
  - Routes can be drawn on plans of the school prepared by the teacher. A selection of route maps could be displayed in different parts of the school, to direct visitors to the headteacher's office, to the hall, or the medical room, etc.

- Use completed directions to make up 'mystery tours', where given the starting point and the route, the children have to work out the eventual destination.
- Survey how many doors had to be gone through during the course of the journey, and how many left and right turns had to be made. Ask the children to complete a grid of their results.
- Plan a walk in the local area as part of topic work, to investigate a local feature, or to gather information; for example, following a route to the local shops, tracing a route to a nearby pond, to carry out a buildings or transport survey. The children should be encouraged to follow the route taken on a large scale map such as an Ordnance Survey scale 1:1250, or 1:2500, stopping at regular intervals to point out landmarks and to make decisions about the directions to take. Take photographs of important landmarks or features as the walk proceeds. These can then be labelled and mapped onto an enlarged map for display.
- Plan a route around a local supermarket on a plan prepared by the teacher. Ask the children to write a shopping list and then devise the most direct and economical pathway, visiting the sections needed.
- Ask the children to choose a place they would like to visit, to plan a journey using public transport and to draw a route map of their intended journey.
- Devise an imaginary route for an ant, a caterpillar, or a spider crawling over a table top, or over your bedroom floor. Plot the creature's route from object to object.
- Orienteering courses can be set up in the classroom or resource area, in the school playground, or further afield in a park, as long as the children can be supervised safely. Provide the children with a map of the school grounds with buildings, fences, walls, trees, grassy areas, climbing frames, and any other significant features marked using conventional symbols. Mark a series of controls numbered 1-20 randomly on the map. Place P.E. cones, skittles or markers (to represent the controls) in the chosen sites in the school grounds.

Each control (i.e. the P.E. cones, skittles, etc.) should be labelled with the appropriate number and with a letter of the alphabet, for example 16A. The children are given the task of visiting each control by reading the map, and collecting the letters they find there. These letters can then be used to complete a crossword puzzle or to solve an anagram compiled by the teacher.
Talk to the children in the classroom before going outside. Encourage them to look closely at the map, to read the key, to locate their present position, and to start planning an economical route from control to control. Ask 'Which control is nearest to us now? Which control do you think is the furthest away? Which number control is close to the playhouse?' Children can work individually or with a partner, where one child holds the map while the other lists the letters as they are collected. Start each group at a different point around the course. The teacher can be positioned at a central point and can observe the strategies that the children are using. Encourage the children to orientate the map as they change direction, and to keep using landmarks as reference points.

- Alternatively, each control could have a coloured pencil at the marker so that a 'colour by number' puzzle could be completed.
- Older children could be involved in more conventional orienteering exercises where each control has a compass bearing which directs them towards the next control marked on the map.

Maps and map making

Discussion

When do we need to use maps? Ask the children to relate their personal experience of using maps. Who else uses maps? Talk about people who use maps in their jobs, for example, road builders, planners, architects, engineers, builders, weather forecasters, tour leaders, lorry drivers, etc.

● Collect different kinds of maps and create a valuable resource for the school. A collection should include a large-scale map of the immediate area (Ordnance Survey 1:1250 or 1:2500) and smaller scale maps (1:10,000, 1:25,000, or 1:50,000) of the more general locality. A range of atlases and globes should also be available for the children to look at. Collect maps and plans of places visited regularly, bus routes, underground maps, road maps and journey planners, tourist maps, museum and gallery floor plans, geological maps, weather maps, navigation charts and star charts. The resource bank should also include plans of the classroom, plans of the school buildings and grounds, together with oblique and vertical aerial photographs of the local area.

● Talk about who would make use of each kind of map. (See photograph above.)

- Talk about how each type of map is specifically designed to serve a different purpose. Compare a detailed street map with a tourist map showing places of interest. Look at the simplicity of the design of an underground or subway map compared to a map showing bus routes (although bus stops and bus guides often have linear type diagrams for quick reference).

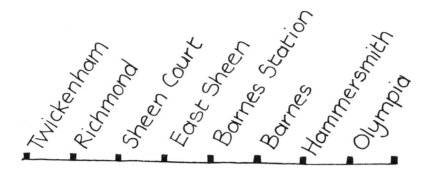

- Look at a globe and ask the children to point out what they can see: areas of land, seas and oceans, mountain ranges, continents, the Equator, the North and the South Pole, the Tropic of Cancer, and the Tropic of Capricorn. Identify your own location. Talk about the northern hemisphere and the southern hemisphere and lines of longitude and latitude. Trace routes from place to place on the globe.
- Talk about the advantages and disadvantages of using a globe. It gives a 'truer' picture of what the world looks like, but a globe cannot be carried around as easily as a folded map. To make a map (a flat representation of the curved surface of the earth) various areas have to be stretched or shrunk. Older children can investigate the different projections used in atlases, and the people who invented them - such as Mercator, Peters, or Robinson.
- Look carefully at the different kinds of maps found in an atlas, and what they show, for example, political, physical and geological details, climatic regions, population density or land use.
- Make a collection of objects that have maps on them. Children will enjoy searching these out. The collection could include stamps, flags, food labels, postcards, badges, souvenirs, mugs, T-shirts, board games, tea towels, weather charts, newspaper articles, road signs, holiday brochures, wine bottles, and jigsaw puzzles.
- Investigate how maps are made and find out about the work of cartographers, surveyors and printers. Look at the work carried out by Ordnance Survey, or the agency responsible for producing maps in your country. Find out about the history of map-making, and research the famous navigators, explorers and pioneers. Some names to look up include Ptolemy, Ortelius, William Roy, Meriwether Lewis and William Clark. Find out about modern techniques including satellite photography and computer technology.
- Look at old maps of your local area. Compare with recent maps to find out how things have changed. List the changes and draw them. Contact the local history society to see if they have old photographs of the area that can be photocopied. Take photographs of the same view in the present day and create a 'Then and Now' display using maps, photographs and perhaps some eyewitness accounts of how the local area has changed.
- Enlarged copies of maps can be produced by copying the map onto an OHP transparency, and projecting it onto large sheets of paper fixed to the wall. Trace the map as it is being projected. Check that your local education authority has a licensing agreement with the Ordnance Survey for maps to be copied for educational purposes.

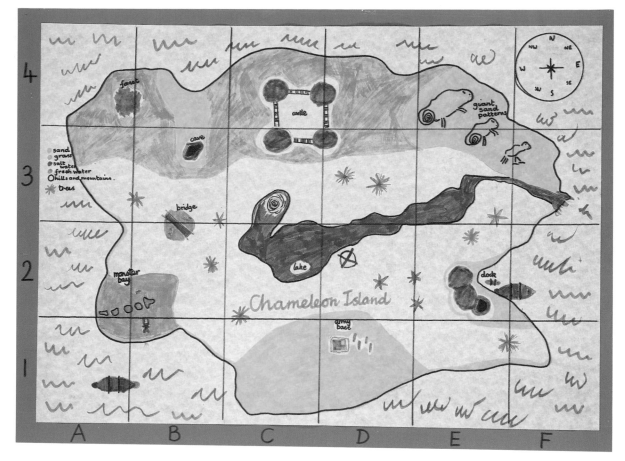

A treasure map

- Town centre plans and shopping precinct maps are a useful resource as they give details of shops and building use in an area.
- Encourage children to always check when a map was made. Point out that maps constantly need to be revised because of changes being made. Perhaps there have been some recent changes to your local area that need to be recorded?

Drawing Maps

- Provide opportunities for very young children to play with a variety of toys including train sets, model farm and zoo animals, play-mats, Lego, and Playmobile figures, and a large sand tray.
- Encourage the children to design and draw their own play-mats depicting a farm, zoo, railway network, roadway, shopping centre or park by providing large sheets of sugar paper, chalks, and large felt-tip pens.
- Paint playground markings around a play house or boat. Include features such as a path, a road, a crossing, a stream with a bridge, stepping stones, a wooded area, islands, cliffs and rocks.
- Children of all ages can draw 'story' maps, mapping the area in which a story, traditional or modern, is set. The maps of the youngest children will be pictorial, but as they gain more experience of working with plans and maps, and of following routes, their representations of features will begin to follow map conventions and they will start to experiment with using symbols. Some ideas for stories:

    Little Red Riding Hood, Hansel and Gretel, The Gingerbread Man.
    Fantastic Mr Fox, Roald Dahl (Puffin); *The Iron Man,* Ted Hughes (Faber and Faber); *The Midnight Fox,* Betsy Byars (Puffin).

Myths and legends from other countries often feature a challenge or journey that takes the characters to different landscapes, for example, The Thunder King (see chapter on Peru), and various Greek myths.

- Picture books that feature 'flight' are a good way to introduce the idea of 'a bird's eye view', for example, *The Gift,* John Prater (Picture Puffin), *Up and Up,* Shirley Hughes (Picture Lions). The closing chapters of *Charlie and the Chocolate Factory,* Roald Dahl (Puffin), can be used as a stimulus for map drawing. Ask the children to draw what Charlie would see through the floor of the Great Glass Elevator as he flies over his home town.

Activities to encourage the development of concepts of perspective
- Lie on a long table or bench and look at objects from above. Ask the children to look carefully and to draw what they see.
- Draw around objects, for example, coins, toys, small P.E. apparatus, bricks and 3D shapes. Ask the children to colour the shapes and talk about the space that the shape takes up.
- Photograph familiar objects from different angles. Play a game of 'guess the object' with the children.
- Ask the children to take rubbings of grids and gratings, and patterns in floor tiles and brick paving to show plan views.
- Place toys or small familiar objects onto an overhead projector. Draw around them on the overlay, and then remove them. Ask the children to guess what the objects were.
- Make a 'lift-the-flap' book. Ask the children to draw a plan view of an object on the outside of each flap, and a picture of the object underneath. The children can then ask their friends to guess the objects and to lift the flaps to see if they were right.
- Prepare an outline plan of the classroom and ask the children to insert furniture and objects in the correct position.
- Study oblique and vertical aerial photographs of the local area. Locate landmarks and compare the photographs with a large scale map covering the same area.
- Tell the story of 'Theseus and the Minotaur' (a Greek myth) and talk about labyrinths and mazes. Collect pictures of mazes (visit one if possible) and give the children a lot of experience in completing maze puzzles. Ask the children to draw their own 2D mazes using grid paper. 3D mazes can be made with match sticks, bricks, construction toys, and Plasticine.
- Design a new layout by drawing a plan for
  a) a classroom
  b) a bedroom
  c) a resource area
  d) an adventure playground
  e) a room in a dolls' house
  f) a supermarket
  g) a shopping centre

- **Draw a signpost map.** First of all, ask the children to draw themselves in the centre of a piece of paper. Then ask them to point to different features of the room, furniture or objects and to draw them in the right position on their plan in relation to themselves. Draw a line to each object, as shown in the line drawing. This activity can be extended to the school grounds and beyond.

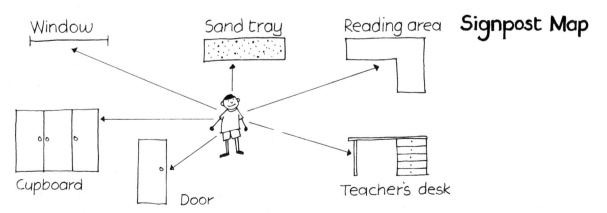

- Develop children's map-drawing skills by providing a prepared map or plan and asking them to extend the map to include the surrounding area.

Using conventional symbols

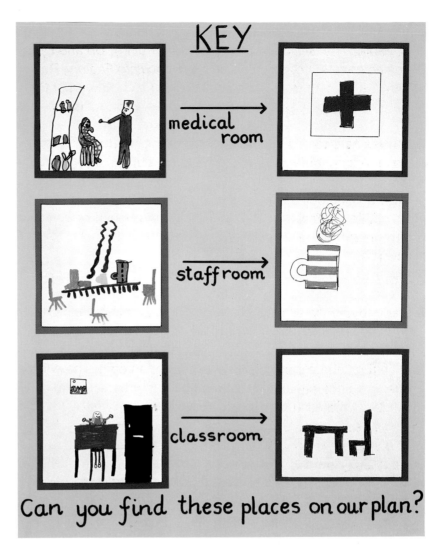

Ask the children to devise their own symbols to add to a prepared sketch map of the school and its grounds. Draw and label a 'key' to explain the symbols used. Posters of these signs could be made to label different areas of the school, for example, the hall, classroom, dining room, resource area and library.

Talk to the children about signs and symbols that we see every day: warning signs, information signs (telephones, tourist office, Post Office, shop signs, public toilets), and road signs.

Discuss how features can be shown on maps - they can be labelled, a picture can be drawn, or a symbol or special sign can be designed to represent the feature. Look at a range of maps and choose some of the most interesting symbols. (Tourist maps have a wide variety.) Make a poster or chart of symbols, together with their meaning, to display in the classroom.

Study a map of the local area and identify the conventional symbols used. Ask the children to locate rivers, forests, roads and railways, mountains, schools, hospitals and churches, and places of interest.

Collect maps from other countries and compare the conventional symbols used. Point out similarities as well as differences. Are any symbols exactly the same?

Design an information pack for a place you have visited. The pack could include details of opening times, how to get there, an historical account of the place, and also a map showing all the main attractions. Look at the different ways that maps are folded, and design your own as a technology challenge.

Look at how maps show the different heights of land. For example, early maps simply showed a drawing of a hill or mountain. Later, 'hachuring' was used - a method of shading the hillside.

Maps today use a more sophisticated form of hill-shading, layer-tinting, spot heights, and contour lines. Explain to the children how contour lines join places of the same height. Study a map and look for steep slopes (where the lines are close together), and look for the use of colour to show the height of the land. Try to find out if there are any 'bench marks' in the neighbourhood. These show exact heights and are used by surveyors, architects and engineers.

Scale and distance - are very difficult concepts, but awareness can be developed in very young children in preparation for accurate scale drawing later.

● Produce life-size plans of hands, feet, objects and shapes by drawing around them. Enlarge and reduce these on a photocopier, and ask the children to order them according to size.

● Use toys, models and household objects to illustrate a discussion about scale. For example, show the children a miniature dolls' house iron, a playhouse toy iron and a real iron.

● Have fun playing with proportions! Ask the children to paint a series of figures of different sizes. Try putting life-size hands and feet onto smaller figures, and vice versa.

● Make it fit. Ask children to draw the same picture on progressively smaller pieces of paper. Start with size A1, A2, A3, A4, A5 and so on.

● Encourage a recognition of the need for scale. Ask each child to draw a picture of themselves, or of their home. Try to fit them onto one piece of paper. Ask: What can we do to make them all fit on? Shall we make just some of them smaller? Reduce all of the pictures using a photocopier.

● Give the children a range of papers with different sized squares. Ask them to draw a 2x2 square on each piece. Colour them and cut them out. Compare the sizes of the drawn shapes.

● Look at maps of the local area of different scales. Talk about large scale maps - what features can you see? Compare with small scale maps, and ask the children: Which map would be better for planning a long journey? Which map should I use for finding a street in my local area?

● Older children can look for the scale written on the map. Explain the relationship between measurements in real-life, and measurements on the map.
Look at architects' drawings of the school if they are available. Take measurements and compare with the scale drawings.

Location: activities involving grid references

● Demonstrate how much easier it is to locate something on a map if a grid of squares is placed over the top and if each square can be identified by number or letter. Show the children a 'treasure map' and ask them to describe where the treasure is hidden (mark with an X or a symbol). Place a piece of acetate over the map, marked with grid lines, and show them how to read the grid reference for the location of the treasure.

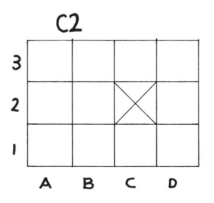

Teach the children to read the letters or numbers along the bottom first. Those are called the eastings. Then the numbers at the sides are read - the northings.
Devise a poster to remind them of this rule. ('Along the corridor and up the stairs')

● Ask the children to design their own treasure maps or games using grid references.

● Look at town centre plans and A-Z street plans and use grid references to locate places and features.

● Look at longitude and latitude lines in an atlas and on a globe. The latitude is always given first, before the longitude. Work out the reference for your nearest city.

Buildings

● As with all elements of this work, it is important that you begin with buildings with which the children are familiar. One way of achieving this is to take the children for a walk in the immediate vicinity of the school. Before you go, establish a list of different types of building. On your return, go through this list with the children, asking them which buildings you saw on your walk. Ask them to describe the building and its purpose.

● Make a display of your walk. Draw the route that you took on large pieces of paper. Provide the children with paper on which to draw one of the buildings that they saw. Talk to the children about where they should position their buildings. For example, ask them if the church was before the dairy. When you have stuck the buildings to the display, add children's writing about the function of each building. (Instead of using children's pictures you can make a display with photographs taken on the walk.)

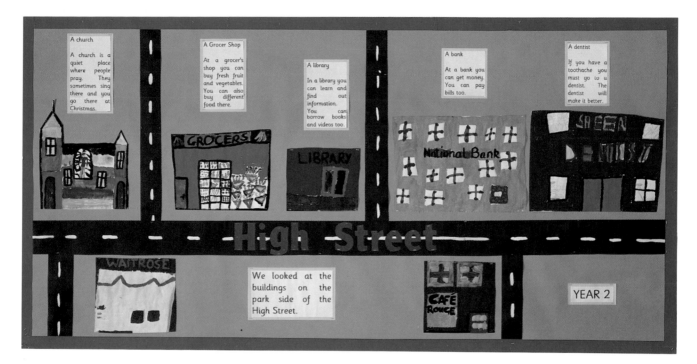

● Initiate a study of the school building. Involve the children in a survey of the school and its accommodation. Ask them to find out what kinds of rooms there are in the school building, how many of each type of room there are, and the function of each room. Collate all the information that the children have discovered. The information may be presented in a variety of forms - in a book 'Our School', as a wall display, or in a series of charts.

classrooms	6
offices	2
toilets	5

● Allow the children to investigate the use of the land surrounding the school - the different play surfaces, the car parking, outside storage area, etc. Position the children in different areas of the surrounding school grounds. Talk to them about what they can see, and ask them to draw, as accurately as possible, their observations. Show the resulting pictures to the whole class and ask the other children to say where they think the child was when he/she drew the picture. Draw a simple plan of the school and the grounds and ask the children to stick the pictures on the appropriate place.

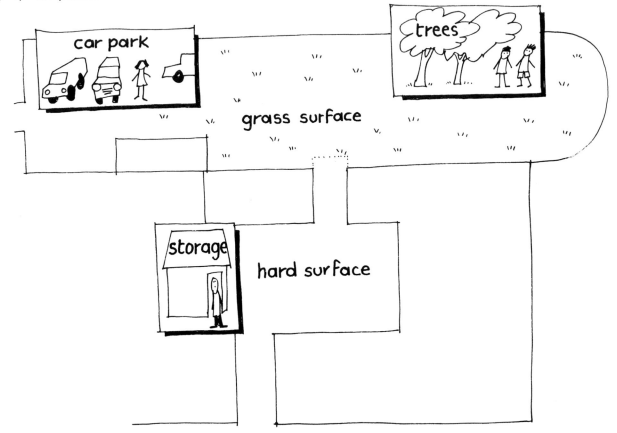

Dwellings

● Ask the children about where they live and what kind of building it is. From this discussion extend the children's understanding about the different kinds of dwellings - flat, maisonette, bungalow, house. Talk about different forms of housing - terraced, semi-detached and detached. Give the children a piece of paper and ask each to draw a picture of where they live. Under the picture, they write a sentence, 'I live in a ....'. They then choose a friend who lives in a different type of dwelling and they draw a picture of that, with a relevant caption, for example, 'Pat lives in a ....'. Allow the children, in pairs, to discuss what is the same and what is different about their dwellings. The pairs report back to the whole class and then record the similarities and differences.

● Show the children pictures of houses and flats. Ask them what materials were used to construct them and why those materials were chosen. **Give the children a drawing of a house with arrows indicating different parts of the building. The children write or draw the appropriate construction material next to the arrows.** Ask them why certain materials are chosen.

● The appropriateness of different materials can be highlighted by telling the story of 'The Three Pigs'. Why were bricks a sensible option for the third pig? What were the disadvantages of straw and sticks? Provide the children with suitable materials to make models or collages of the three houses and caption them with reasons for and against choosing the materials.
Include other stories and poems about unusual houses or dwellings - 'The Old Woman who Lived in a Shoe' and the gingerbread house in 'Hansel and Gretel' are good examples, and lend themselves to interesting display work.

● Investigate how construction materials are made. Collect relevant information books for this work. With the children, make recipe cards for the different materials.

> ## Recipe for glass
>
> **Ingredients:**
>
> sand
> limestone
> soda ash
> recycled glass
>
> lots of heat

● Obtain architect's drawings of a building. Draw the children's attention to different aspects of the drawing and introduce certain technical terms - elevation, plan, etc. Ask the children to draw a plan of a building or house that they will then be required to make with a constructional kit. Display the resulting models with the children's plans. **Encourage the children to evaluate their plans and models,** noting differences between the original plan and the resulting model, and why these differences occurred.

I had to make a flat roof. The pointed one was too difficult.

● Collect pictures of houses in different parts of the world. Ask the children and their families if they have any pictures of houses from their journeys or holidays to different countries for your display. Look at the pictures carefully with the children. Discuss why the houses have different appearances in different parts of the world. Consider climatic conditions - long sloping roofs in countries where there is likely to be a lot of snow, small windows (or ones with shutters) in hot countries; the availability of land space - skyscrapers on restricted land spaces in inner cities; and economic conditions - the comparison of wealthy and poor people's dwellings. It is important when talking to the children that you avoid any romantic or cultural stereotypes.

● Talk about animals' dwellings. The children will probably know the names of certain animals' homes, for example, stable, kennel and sty. Introduce them to some new ones and describe them, what they are made of and where they are found. Distinguish between those that the animals make themselves and those that are made by people to accommodate animals. Provide the children with a variety of collage materials and ask them to make pictures of different types of animals' homes. Display the pictures with suitable captions.

ANIMAL HOMES

A horse lives in a stable. | A pig lives in a sty. | A dog lives in a kennel.

Shops
● Discuss with the children the shops in the immediate vicinity of the school and their homes. Talk about what the shops sell. Ask the children which shops they and their families visit. **Devise with the children a simple questionnaire form** to find out where their families tend to do most of their food shopping. Let the children take the forms home for a family representative to complete.

I do most of my shopping at

-the local shops ☐

- a superstore ☐

signed _____

When the children bring back the completed forms, ask them to count the number of families that indicate that they use superstores and those who use smaller local shops. Make a graph of the results. Talk to the children about the differences between superstores and local shops - where they are located, what they sell, when they are open, what they have heard their families say about the prices, etc. **Ask one group of children to paint a picture of a superstore and another group to paint a small specialist shop.** All the other children write a sentence describing one of them. Display the sentences under the relevant picture.

● This work is enhanced by visits to a superstore and local shops. Contact the shops before the visit to ask if they would agree for the children to visit the loading bays, warehouses, storerooms and offices attached to the store. Such visits will develop a more sophisticated appreciation of the work of the shops.

If you are able to take the children on a visit to a shop, take the opportunity to initiate an enquiry with the children on where some of the products come from. Choose one shelf or area of the shop. The canned fruit and vegetables section is a good one to choose. Talk to the children about the different products that they can find on the shelves. Introduce them to any new or unusual vegetables or fruits. Examine, with the children, the labels on the cans. Show them where they are likely to find certain pieces of information and particularly the country of origin for the product. Ask the children to record the information 'type of vegetable/fruit' and 'country'.

● When you return to school, use a large map of the world with the children and find the countries that the children recorded from their investigations. **Get the children to draw a picture of the fruits and vegetables on small pieces of paper. Put the map on the wall and, using strips of paper and drawing pins, indicate where the various products came from.**

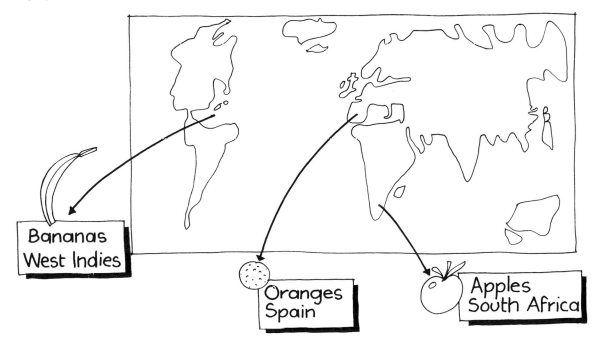

● Investigate with the children how the product reaches this country. Tell the story of the harvesting of the crop; the preserving; the transportation to the docks, across the sea and its journey from the docks to warehouses and, finally, to the shops. Make a picture flow diagram of the journey with the children.

People pick the bananas → People pack the bananas → The boxes go on ships. The ships sail to the U.K. → The boxes are put on lorries which go to shops.

● With some children it may be appropriate to explore the types of fruit and vegetables that come from different countries and how climatic features determine the varieties of produce grown.
Make lists of fruit and vegetables that grow in this country and those that do not.
Collect pictures and divide these into sets.

grapes   blueberries

peppers   limes   pineapples   lychees

cumquats

Fruit and vegetables not often grown in this country.

root ginger

bananas   melons   figs   kiwi fruit

oranges   avocados

lemons

● If you are unable to visit a shop, it is still possible to complete this exercise by asking the children and your colleagues to bring to school as many different examples of canned fruit and vegetables as possible.

Factories

Establish with the children the principle of how factories work - the transformation of raw materials into a final product.

● Look around the classroom. Ask the children to identify all the things that they can see that would have been made in a factory. Gather together a collection of these articles. Talk about the raw materials that would have been needed to make some of the articles. **Write down the raw materials under the children's drawings of your collected items.**

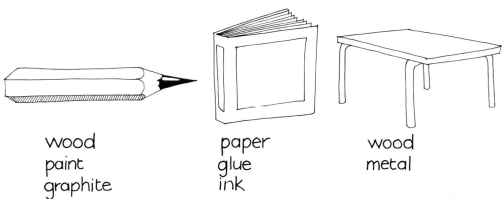

wood
paint
graphite

paper
glue
ink

wood
metal

● Manufacturing processes frequently have very clear sequences. Choose one or two procedures to explore in detail with the children. (Your choice may be influenced by local factories and industries.) There are many information books that support this work.

● Set up a factory in the classroom. Discuss with the children what they want to produce. The choice must take into account practical restrictions of the classroom.
One possible idea is to print greetings cards. Talk to the children about all the different elements of the task - the design, the preparation of the materials (cutting card, etc.), the printing, the packaging and the distribution.
Put the children into appropriately sized groups and assign the groups specific tasks. Allow the groups time to think of ways of making their aspect of the process as efficient as possible. Let the children determine the order in which the elements have to be undertaken. **Take photographs of the children engaged in each of the tasks.**
When the children have finished the process, talk to them about which elements they felt were successful and ways in which the whole process or aspects could have been improved.
Make a display using the photographs you took of the whole procedure. The children write captions to explain the element that they were responsible for.

Sasha and Lei drew the design.

Tyrone cut the card.

Abdul did the printing.

● Develop this activity by including aspects of advertising and marketing. Ask the children how they could sell their cards. Talk about advertising. Show them examples of different advertisements. Let the children consider the things that they would have to include on posters that they were making to publicise their greetings cards - the price, where to buy them, etc. Get all the children to do rough sketches of a poster design. Choose with the children the poster or posters that are most effective and allow the children who drew these to make full-sized versions of their designs.

The children may wish to design leaflets to advertise their products as well.

Discuss the price that the children are going to charge for the packs of cards. Allow some children to do some market research - how much do cards cost in shops? Some children can work out the cost of production, including the cost of the raw materials. Use this information with the class to help decide the final product cost.

If the class do market their product, ask a small group of children to keep simple accounts of the exercise. The children may decide to send any profits to a charity.

● Keep a diary with the children of the story of their factory.

● One of the side effects of some industrial processes is pollution. Talk to the children about some of the types of pollution - air pollution, river and sea pollution and disposal of solid waste. Discuss ways in which some of these problems can be addressed.

● Ask the children to think of the waste products from the manufacturing exercise that they engaged in. Were there any ways in which they could have reduced the waste? What are the implications of, say, wasting paper? How is the waste that they created disposed of?

Work and leisure

Starting Point

Talk to the children about the words *work* and *leisure.* Ask them what they think the words mean. For the children, work may mean being in school, and leisure when they are at home. Extend the discussion to activities they enjoy, whether in school or at home. Ask if they have to do jobs at home. It may be possible to arrive at a definition that works for them. Discuss how they consider adults might think about work and leisure. Ask if they think being paid for an activity means it's work, and if it's unpaid it's leisure.

LEISURE

Ask the children what they do in their leisure time. **Record the activities on a large piece of paper.**

Depending on the list, ask the children to begin to classify them. Possible headings might include:

- indoor - outdoor
- active - non-active
- need other people - done alone
- regularly - occasionally
- can be done all year - only at certain times of the year
- organised by others - organised by self

Brownies
Cycling
Reading
Swimming
Fishing
Computer Games
Watch T.V.
Playing with dolls
Playing Lego
Majorettes.

Give groups of children a large sheet of paper and ask each group to illustrate one of the categories (see photograph above).

- Ask individual children to prepare a short talk on a special hobby or activity. It could be illustrated with pictures or objects, etc.
- Ask individual children to set up an exhibition of their hobbies, for example, Lego building, puppets, stamp collection or other collections, items used in the majorettes, etc.
- Ask the children to write a story that involves their activity or favourite pastime.
- Ask individual children or a group of children to give a demonstration of something they take part in, for example, drama group, Cubs or Brownies, playing a card or board game.

- Ask individual children or a group of children to make a book about their hobby, one that would help others to take part in it.

- Ask a group of children to design a new game or a piece of equipment that could be used for a hobby or activity.
- **Ask individuals or a group to design an outfit to wear for a particular activity,** for example, going sledging in the snow, to wear at a football match, for cycling, going fishing, etc.

- Make a class graph of the favourite activities. These could be classified as before, for example,
  Our Favourite Indoor Activities, Favourite Activities in the Winter, Activities We Do with Others, etc.

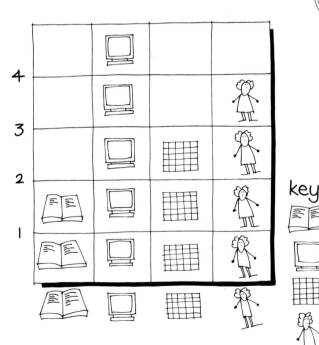

key

☐ – Reading

☐ – Computer Games

☐ – Board Games

☐ – Playing with dolls

AN ACTIVITY DAY

To introduce new activities to children and give them an opportunity to try them out, organise an Activity Day for the class. It will be necessary to have access to at least two indoor rooms and an outside area. There may be parents, governors or friends of the school who would be willing to come for the day to help with an activity, to demonstrate a new skill, play a game or read to the children.

Give the children the list of possible activities and ask them to choose four to take part in during the day. Encourage them to try at least one completely new activity.

Take photographs throughout the day of all the activities to make an exhibition in the classroom. Many of the items made during the day can also be used for an exhibition. It may also be possible to tape record some items such as the play reading, stories and poems that have been written, skipping chants, etc. to serve as a reminder of the day.

Drama	Modelling	Board Games	Cycling
Jennifer	Peter Carol	Tina Carol	John
David	Mark	Stuart	Sam
Anna	Matthew	Anna	Tina
Peter	Tina	David	Jennifer

POSSIBLE ACTIVITIES

INDOORS

Play reading and drama activity: It is helpful to have dressing-up clothes and make-up available.

Knitting and Sewing: This could be fairly formal, teaching the children to get started with the basic skills. Have available plenty of wool, knitting needles, various plain fabrics, sewing needles, scissors and thread.

Model-making: Have available a variety of card, paper, plastic, wood, straw, ribbons, paint, brushes, small hand tools, glue and paste, fabrics, etc.

Board Games: Chess, Draughts, Ludo, Junior Scrabble, Snakes and Ladders, etc.

Pottery: You would need clay or other modelling material. Have available paint, brushes, various scrapers and modelling tools, varnish.

Extended Writing activity: Creative writing, writing a story book for younger children, play writing, poetry, etc.

OUTDOORS

Natural History: A study of the trees, plants, signs of animals and birds within the vicinity of the school. The children could make sketches, drawings, paintings, etc. It is helpful to have a good selection of easy-to-use reference books for identifying their findings, some magnifying glasses, binoculars and containers for samples of leaves, plants, etc.

Skipping Games: These can be collective or individual. Encourage the children to use rhymes and chants. They could make up their own or use traditional ones. Members of the older generation may be able to teach the children ones they used to say.

Ball Skills: Various ball handling skills using all sizes of balls to catch, dribble, kick, throw, roll, shoot at a goal or net, etc.

Cycling: For children who can bring a bike to school: road safety work, stunts (for BMX bikes), how to check their bikes for safety, etc.

Swimming: Games and activities.

Country Dancing: Simple traditional dancing from either this country or elsewhere, depending on the availability of adults to teach the children.

WORK

Read to the children the poem on the facing page, and ask them to illustrate all the verses. Ask each child or small groups of children to write a further verse in the same style using occupations of their own choice.

Discuss with the children any other occupations they know about, or their ideas of what they may do when they leave school.

It would be helpful to have a collection of books and leaflets that describe different occupations. The local Careers Service can usually provide a great deal of information, but the children would need help to read it.

An A to Z of Jobs

● List the alphabet on a board or large piece of paper. Ask the children to think of as many jobs as they can that start with each of the letters, for example,

A - architect, airline pilot, accountant, artist, actor

B - baker, band leader, brewer, barrister, builder, boat builder, bricklayer

C - carpet layer, computer programmer, composer, conductor, carpenter, cook, chef, cameraman, civil engineer

D - dentist, doctor, driving instructor, designer, dancer

E - engineer, engraver, entomologist, electrician, entertainer

F - fire fighter, forester, florist, film director, furniture designer/maker, fashion designer

G - garage owner, goldsmith, grocer, graphic designer, gardener

H - housekeeper, hotelier, house decorator

I - inspector, illustrator, inventor

J - journalist, judge, juggler, jeweller, jockey

K - key-cutter, knitter

L - lorry driver, lifesaver, librarian, locksmith

M - machinist, musician, miner, mechanic, Member of Parliament

N - nurse, nursery nurse

O - opera singer

P - policeman, plasterer, printer, plumber, photographer, potter, publisher

Q - quantity surveyor

R - radiographer, referee

S - sailor, shepherd, solicitor, scientist, shop assistant, secretary, singer, shopkeeper

T - teacher, travel agent, truck driver, typist

U - umpire, undertaker

V - vet, van driver, violinist

W - waiter, waitress, window cleaner

X - xylophone player

Y - yachtsman

Z - zoo keeper

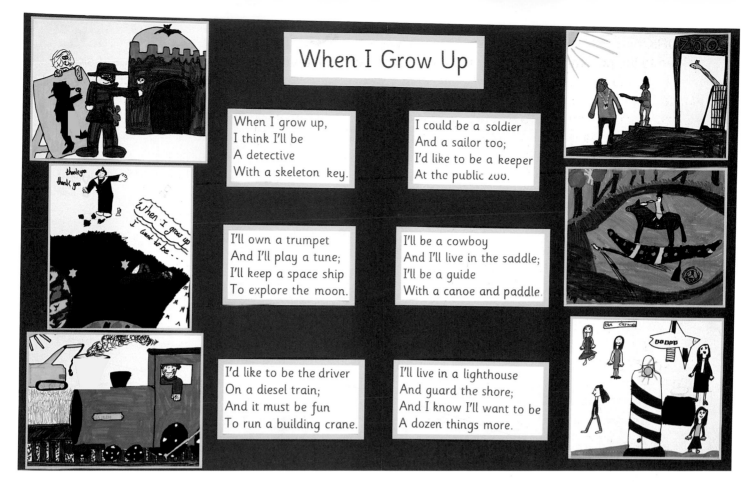

When I Grow Up

When I grow up,
I think I'll be
A detective
With a skeleton key.

I could be a soldier
And a sailor too;
I'd like to be a keeper
At the public zoo.

I'll own a trumpet
And I'll play a tune;
I'll keep a space ship
To explore the moon.

I'll be a cowboy
And I'll live in the saddle;
I'll be a guide
With a canoe and paddle.

I'd like to be the driver
On a diesel train;
And it must be fun
To run a building crane.

I'll live in a lighthouse
And guard the shore;
And I know I'll want to be
A dozen things more.

Ask small groups of children to draw and write one or two sentences about some of the occupations listed on the facing page. These can be made into a classroom display or bound together to make a class book.

A fireman helps to put out fires.

A nurse works in a hospital.

A journalist writes for a newspaper.

- Talk to the children about public services, especially the ones they are most likely to have some experience of, for example, police, nurses and doctors, ambulance drivers, fire fighters, etc.
- Help the children to write to the Local Council for further information about the services that are provided by them. Choose one of the services and discuss with the children what sort of jobs the people employed might have, for example:
Highways Department would need: civil engineers, drivers, labourers, clerical workers, etc.
Housing Department would need: bricklayers, carpenters, electricians, architects, quantity surveyors, plumbers, etc.

Follow this up by inviting someone from a department to talk to the children about the work that is undertaken and the people they employ.

Prior to a visit by a speaker, help the children to write a list of questions they would like to have answered, for example:

1. How many people are employed by the department?
2. What sort of jobs do they have?
3. What is the usual type of work they have to deal with?
4. How do they know what work is required?
5. What is the most difficult thing they have had to do?
6. How do the employees travel to work?
7. Have there been any changes to the work they do?
8. Why have these changes come about?

It may be possible to follow this up with a visit to a site or local offices so the children can see at first hand the work in action.

● Find out where the following are, and mark on a map of the local area: Police Station, Fire Station, Hospital, Doctor's Surgery, Local Council Offices, Ambulance Station, Town Hall, etc.

● Study architects' plans for a new house or estate, or the school buildings.

● Using the list of occupations, classify them in various ways, e.g. manual - non-manual, indoor - outdoor, active - sedentary, meet the public - do not meet the public, manufacturing - service industry - other.

● Individual children interview parent, grandparent or other relatives about their work. Encourage the children to ask in particular: how the job has changed, if they have had the job since leaving school, what the main aspects of the job are, what they like about the job, what they dislike, etc.

Transport

Talk to the children about the word transport. Through this discussion, reach a definition of the word - something that takes you from one place to another.

● Once you have agreed a definition, ask the children to think of as many different examples as they can. They may initially concentrate on road transport but broaden the discussion to include water and air transport. As the children suggest different types of transport write them down on a large piece of paper. When you have completed the list, go through it again with the children and let them choose one or two types to draw. Support this work by providing the children with reference books about transport to enable them to check details for their drawings. Ask the children to cut out their drawings.

Gather the children together with all their pictures. Place some P.E. hoops on the floor and tell the children that you want them to sort the types of transport in as many different ways as possible. The criteria could include:
  - number of wheels
  - whether the vehicle has a motor or not
  - whether it travels in the air, on land or water
  - how it is used - commercially, for leisure or for convenience.

The children will discover that, using some criteria, certain vehicles can go in more than one set. Tell the children that you want them to choose one criterion to display on the wall. Allow them to choose which criterion to use. Provide the children with different coloured paper for the sets and ask them to place the pictures in the appropriate set. (See photograph above.)

- Discuss with the children the types of transport listed, and whether they have ever travelled on these. Ask them when they did and where they were going. From this discussion draw out more details and information about the transportation, for example, why people use air travel to travel long distances. **Make a bar graph of the numbers of children who have used different forms of transport.**

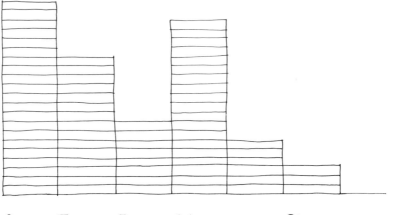

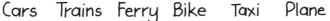

Cars   Trains   Ferry   Bike   Taxi   Plane

Concentrate on different types of transport.

Road Transport

- Talk to the children about all the different kinds of transport that you can find on the roads. Ask the children to describe the vehicles and their purpose. Allow the children to choose a vehicle and ask them to draw them. With a small group of children, make a long road. This may be painted or cut out of paper. Cut out the children's drawings and glue them on to the road. Discuss with the children where their vehicles might be going or coming from, and then ask them to draw the possible destinations. Stick these on the display. Gather the children around the display. Ask them what other things they would expect to see on or near a road - road signs, road markings, pedestrian crossings, etc. Children draw these to add to their picture. Write, or ask the children to write, appropriate captions for the display.

The car is going to to the shops.

The tanker is going to the petrol station

The lorry is going to the factory

The tractor is going to the farm

Conducting a Traffic Survey

- Arrange a short outing with the children to observe the types of road transport in your locality. Before you go, talk to the children about what types of transport they are likely to see. Tell them that you are going to do a survey of the transport. Ask them to predict what form of transport they expect to see most of, and the reasons behind their predictions. Take a note of the estimations. Teach the children how to tally to record their information by marking down the types of transport in groups of five. Prepare some data collection sheets for the children to use.

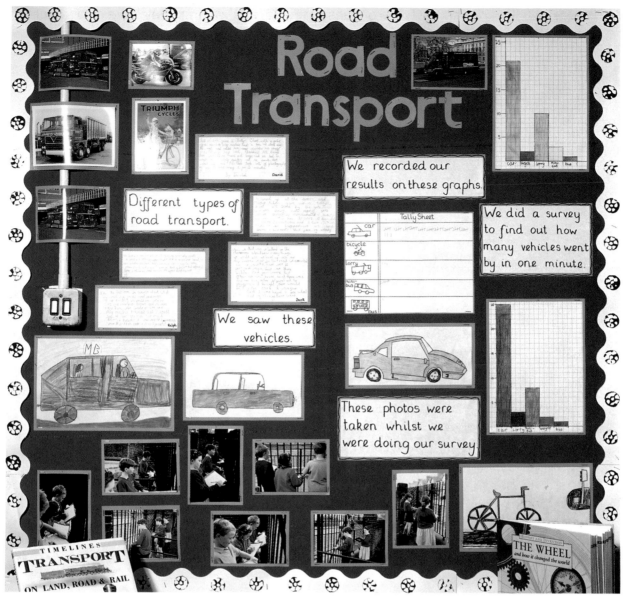

Display - Traffic Survey

Choose a safe place near the school where the children can collect the data. If you have a suitable number of adult supervisors, groups of children could survey different roads. Ensure that the children are aware of the safety implications of being near roads. Collect the data over a short period of time, five or ten minutes. If you allow too long a time the children will have too much information.

When you return to the school, ask the children to summarise the information that they have collected. How many cars passed in that time, how many tankers, lorries, etc.?

Compare the results with the children's predictions. Discuss their findings and, through your questioning, encourage them to postulate reasons behind their findings. Their knowledge of the locality may help them explain some of the findings, for example, a local factory might explain a high proportion of lorries, or a nearby farm might account for a number of agricultural vehicles.

Ask the children to record what they did and what they discovered. Some children write short accounts of the expedition and others record the findings (these can be displayed by graphs or charts). Include examples of the children's tally sheets. Illustrate the resulting display with children's drawings or with photographs that you took of the children at work.

● This activity can be developed by repeating the exercise at different times of the day and comparing the results. The children are asked to explain the differences that they discover.

● Talk with the children about different kinds of roads - motorways, main roads, lanes etc. Show the children examples of maps and explain the way in which different roads are denoted on the maps. Ask the children to invent simple maps with three or four imaginary towns or villages on them, joined by a variety of roads. Once they have completed their maps, get the children to ask a friend how you get from one location to another. These questions can be asked orally, or written down requiring a written response.

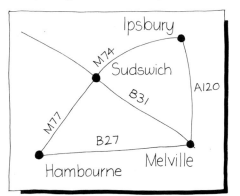

How do you get from Ipsbury to Melville?

The children's maps can be extended by talking about how railways are symbolised on maps. Explain that railways only tend to run between large centres of population.

● Explain to the children the difference between public and private transport. Ask them to think of examples of both categories. Make a display for the classroom based on public transport. **Ask the children to bring to school artefacts connected with public transport - tickets, timetables, etc.** Some children can write to bus, coach or rail organisations asking for publicity material.

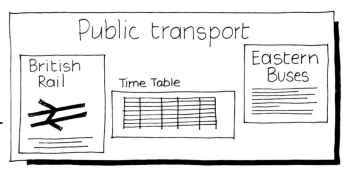

● Choose a simple timetable and explain to the children how it works. (This activity requires the children to have a basic understanding of the twenty-four hour clock.) Refer the children to the maps that they drew and ask them to tell you what public transport serves their towns. Tell them that the service runs four times a day and ask them to draw up a service timetable. They will have to consider how long the journey takes, and the turn around time. The children then determine the fares for the different stages of the journey and make publicity leaflets or posters for their company. Ask them to think of reasons why it is desirable to travel in that particular way.

TRANSPORT

- Children enjoy making models of different types of transport using a range of commercially available construction kits. Display of the children's models is made more interesting by making, with the children, a three-dimensional landscape using, for example, papier mâché. This landscape could include land, sea and rivers to permit the children to construct a number of different vehicles.

Allow the children to investigate the properties of wheeled models under different conditions. Ask them to make a simple wheeled trailer. Provide them with a suitable piece of wood to make a ramp. Let them investigate how far the vehicle runs with the ramp at different gradients or with the trailer loaded with a heavy substance, such as Plasticine. Encourage the children to predict what might happen and then to test their theories. Help the children to record their findings accurately.

- **Consider the people whose jobs are connected with transport.** These will include not only the drivers but those people who maintain the vehicles, sell tickets, etc. Arrange the children in small groups and let them choose a type of transport. One child draws the vehicle and other children draw the associated workers. Display the children's work by placing the vehicle in the centre with arrows connecting the workers.

If it is possible, ask someone who works in transport to come to the school so that the children can ask relevant questions. Before the visit, prepare with the children the questions that they wish to ask.

● Work on transport is ideally suited to trips out of school. You may be fortunate and have a transport museum in the vicinity. If this is the case then it would be appropriate to work with the children to investigate the differences between old-fashioned and contemporary transport. It is more likely that there will be a bus station or a railway station which it is possible to visit. When planning the visit, see how many forms of transport you can use to reach your destination. Involve the children in the planning. If it is possible to use a number of different types of transport, examine the timetables and investigate the costs of the tickets (ask the children to work out the total cost).

On your return from the expedition, make a book with the children about the journey.
Include examples of the tickets and timetables that you needed, the calculations of the costs, children's drawings and writing about the visit, photographs that you took and information that the children discovered when they reached the destination. Allow children to tape the story of the journey.

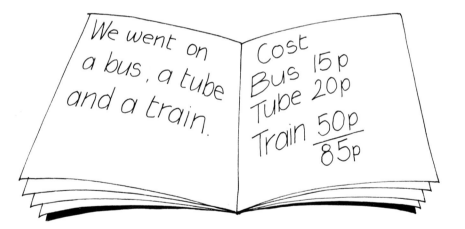

● There are a number of songs, rhymes and poems that support the work on transport.

Food and farming

A study of farming helps children to begin to understand how the food they eat is produced and how different geographical areas are utilised in the production of food.

● A good starting point is the children's lunch, either a packed lunch or a school dinner. Have a good selection of books on farming, cookery (for helping to identify ingredients) and, if possible, food processing, available for the children to use.

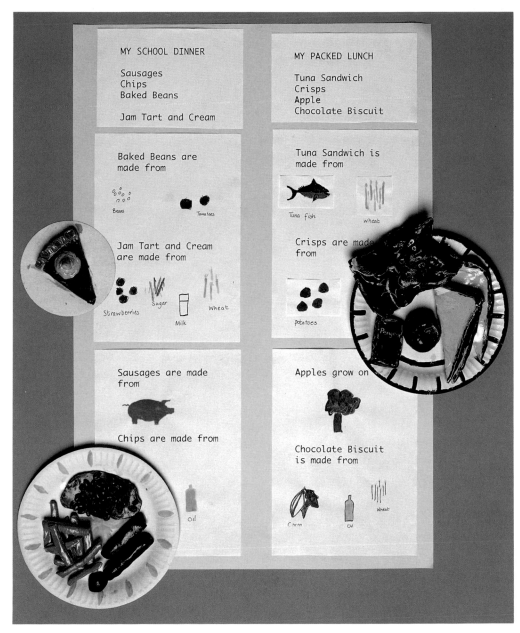

● Ask the children to list what they have had for lunch, or their favourite dinner. Ask them to keep any packaging that contained food items (for example, crisp packets). Ask them to try to discover the main ingredients of each item, for example, crisps - potatoes, salt, flavouring; biscuits - flour, vegetable oil, salt, sugar, cocoa, etc.
Discuss with the children where they think the various ingredients come from and how they might be produced. They might have gardens at home, or have seen crops in the fields or allotments where they live.
● Ask the children to draw or model their meal.
● Research the raw ingredients of the meal (see photograph above).

● Classify the food into the following categories: animal or vegetable.
● Find out whether items are produced in this country or abroad.
● Look at a world map and find the countries where some of the food originates.
● Make a collection of food labels and packaging. Make a display of the collection with more information about what the raw ingredients are, and where they have come from.

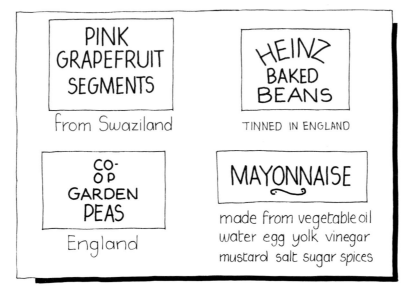

PINK GRAPEFRUIT SEGMENTS

From Swaziland

HEINZ BAKED BEANS

TINNED IN ENGLAND

CO-OP GARDEN PEAS

England

MAYONNAISE

made from vegetable oil water egg yolk vinegar mustard salt sugar spices

● Organise small groups of children to undertake cooking. The children could list the raw ingredients, find out where they have come from, note how food changes when cooked, and how food changes when combined with other ingredients.
This could be followed up by asking other members of the class to taste the items prepared and asking them to guess what they are made from.

● Interview the school cook about the ingredients used in school lunches. They could ask the following:
Where does the food come from?
How is it cooked?
How long can it be stored?
How should it be stored?
How is it prepared?
What happens to the waste/leftovers? etc.

A FARM VISIT
Arrange and plan for the class to visit a farm. The type of farm will depend on the area, but if at all possible try to find a mixed farm that has a variety of activities for the children to observe. The aim of such a visit is to give the children firs-thand experience of farm life and to see some of the daily or seasonal routines in action. The day should give them a reference point for the follow-up activities once back in the classroom.
Discuss with the children, prior to the visit, the things they are likely to see, and introduce a vocabulary of terms they might hear. Have a good collection of books on farming available for the children to use for reference.

Vocabulary
Dairy, arable, pasture, meadow, headland, crops, ploughing, rotation, drilling, cultivation, harvesting, fertiliser, silage, pests, weeds, spraying, drainage, fallow, tractor, combine harvester, plough, cultivator, intensive, cow, bull, calf, bullock, pig, sow, piglet, weaner, sheep, ewe, lamb, ram, bedding, stable, milking parlour, silo, grain store, milk tanker.

This is a field of wheat. It is ready to be cut. The farmer uses a combine harvester to cut it. The grain is used to make flour.

- by Emily and Louise.

This is sugar beet. It will go to the factory and be made into sugar. The rest is used to feed animals.

by Sam and Robert.

This is linseed. It has blue flowers but they have gone now. It is turned into oil.

by Ruth and Gemma.

FARM VISIT

This is a field of rape. It is all dry. In the spring it has bright yellow flowers. It is used for making oil. The oil is used in paint and cooking.

by Matthew and Tom.

We saw a field of horse beans. The farmer grows them to sell. They use them to feed animals.

Joe and David.

This is a field of barley. It will soon be cut. It is used for making beer and to feed pigs.

by George and Tanya

- The adults with the children could be responsible for keeping brief notes for later reference. Try to note the following:

  Crops - what is grown, when sown (drilled) and harvested, care during the season, rotation of crops, where marketed, what they are used for.

  Animals - which animals, daily routine to look after them, where they are kept, feeding practices, uses, marketing.

  Buildings - use of the various buildings, cleaning and maintenance routines, materials used.

  Machinery - what machinery is owned, its uses, where stored.

  People - how many, their jobs, working hours, skills needed, seasonal activities.

- If a camera is available this is an excellent way to record the visit and to assist the work of the children back in class.

- During the visit, the main tasks for the children are to look and listen, but they could certainly draw some of the things they see.

- It may be possible to collect samples of various items, for example, wood, seeds of crops, examples of crops, animal feed, bedding straw, soil samples from different fields.

- Try to make a rough sketch of the farm layout, noting the main buildings, the fields, rivers, streams, ponds, farmhouse, access to road, etc.

Follow-up Activities
● Make a large collage of the farm. Draw an outline plan of the farm and ask groups of children to draw or paint different parts of it.
● Find the farm on a map of the area. (Ordnance Survey 1:25000 is suitable for this purpose.) Ask the children to find any rivers, streams, ponds, etc. They may be able to outline and shade in the whole farm. Include the map in the classroom display. On a smaller scale map find the places where the farm produce is sent, and trace the route.

Making a model of the farm
● A large baseboard is required for this work. Drawn an outline of the farm on to the baseboard. Ask the children to make the following:

Buildings - use thin card and corrugated card, paint in appropriate colours.

Rivers, streams, ponds - use blue shiny paper.

Roadways, tracks, etc. - either paint on to the baseboard or use sand stuck on to the board.

Trees and hedges - use cotton wool dyed green or commercial models.

Fields - grow mustard, cress, beanshoots on lint, to represent different crops and grass.

For fallow fields, use soil stuck to the board.

Animals - model from Plasticine or clay, or use toy animals.

Machinery - ask the children to bring in any toys they may have.

Animal housing, roofs, etc. - straw.

It is worth looking at one or two basic farm products in more detail, in particular looking at the various processes that are involved once the produce leaves the farm.

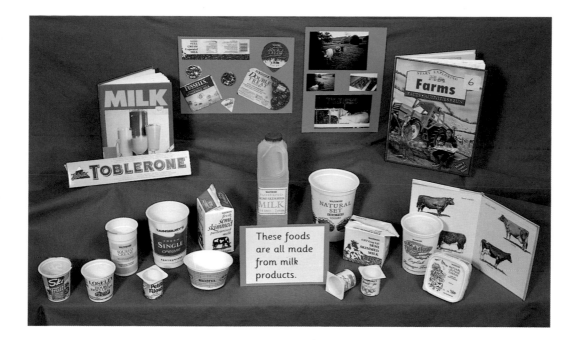

These foods are all made from milk products.

Milk

Milk is used as the basis for many familiar products, for example, cheese, butter, yoghurt, ice-cream, cream, milk puddings, etc., and there are several different types of milk commonly sold in shops, for example, full cream, skimmed, condensed, evaporated, long life, etc.

Discuss with the children the types of milk and milk products they know about. List as many as possible. A visit to a local shop or supermarket will provide a longer list. Ask small groups of children to discover more about how these products are made by using suitable reference books and writing to the manufacturers for more information.

Cereals

Ask the children to list all the different types of cereals frequently grown in this country, for example, wheat, rye, barley, oats. If possible, obtain a small sample of some of these.

Using reference books, ask the children to draw, as accurately as possible, each of the plants. Ask the children to write a brief explanation of what they have drawn.

Further Activities

● **Make a diagram of the farming year** for crop cultivation, for example, drilling, weeding, spraying, watering, harvesting, selling, ploughing.

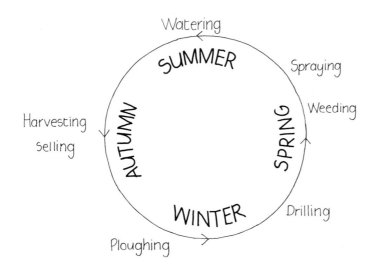

● Make a diagram of crop rotation over a four year cycle.

● Make a list of all the machinery used on a farm, draw the machinery, or find as many pictures as possible from farming magazines and catalogues. Ask the children to write a few sentences for each picture, to give the name of the machine and its use.

● **Draw a cartoon strip to show a typical day's work on a farm in various seasons.** The children should make notes first using any information from the visit, supplemented by using reference books.

WINTER

● Make accurate drawings of any crops the children saw. They should use any samples they brought back from the visit.

● Make some bread or bread rolls. The following recipe will make two small loaves.

> 15g fresh yeast, or 1½ teaspoons dried yeast
> 1 level teaspoon caster sugar
> about 300ml tepid water
> 450g strong plain flour
> 1 level teaspoon salt

Method: Blend the fresh yeast with the water. If using dried yeast, dissolve the sugar in the water, sprinkle the yeast over and leave until frothy. Mix the flour and the salt, make a well in the centre and add the yeast liquid. Mix to a dough, adding more water if necessary. Turn on to a floured board and knead for about five minutes until smooth. Divide the dough into two portions and put into two small bread tins. Put the tins into lightly oiled polythene bags and allow to rise in a warm place until the dough fills the tins and springs back when lightly pressed. Bake at 230°C (450°F, Gas Mark 8) for 30 to 40 minutes. If the dough is made into rolls, bake for 15 to 20 minutes.

Ask the children to describe what has happened to the flour, and the changes that have taken place.

● **Ask the children to list as many ways as possible of preserving food,** for example, canning, freezing, bottling, drying, smoking, pickling, etc. Ask them to draw or model an example of each type.

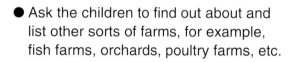

Pickled onions   Smoked bacon   Bottled beetroot   Dried herbs

● Ask the children to find out about and list other sorts of farms, for example, fish farms, orchards, poultry farms, etc.

● **Ask groups of children to make scarecrows,** using whatever scrap materials are available. They could be life-size or miniature. **The children could write stories about their scarecrows.** The stories could be mounted into a class book for others to read.

Water

Discussion/Starting Point

● Ask the children what they have used water for today. They will probably mention the following: washing themselves, cleaning their teeth, having a drink, giving water to a pet, flushing the toilet, washing the dishes.

● Extend the discussion by asking what other uses they can think of, either at home or in school, for example:

in cooking, watering plants in the house or garden, washing clothes either in a washing machine or by hand or at the launderette, washing a car or bike, keeping fish, swimming, water skiing, diving, boat trips, model boats, etc.

● Collect all the ideas together and write them on a large piece of paper. On another large piece of paper write the following headings:

WASHING   COOKING   DRINKING   GROWING   PLAYING

Divide the children into five groups and provide each child with paper. Give each group a heading and ask the members of the group to draw pictures of as many things as possible that fit into their category.

Mount each group's pictures on to separate large pieces of paper, which could be in the shape of a raindrop. (See photograph on facing page.)

Activities

● Collect a variety of materials: wool, cotton, nylon, polyester, velvet, silk, etc. Ask the children to say which they think would dry the fastest. Get the children to wash the fabrics and place them to dry initially in the same place. Ask the children to time how long each fabric takes to dry. Record the results in a graph. This can be developed further by washing several pieces of the same fabric (choosing one that dries fairly quickly), and drying it in different places, for example, in the classroom, outside on a windy day, in a cupboard, flat on a shelf, etc. Again, record the results on a graph.

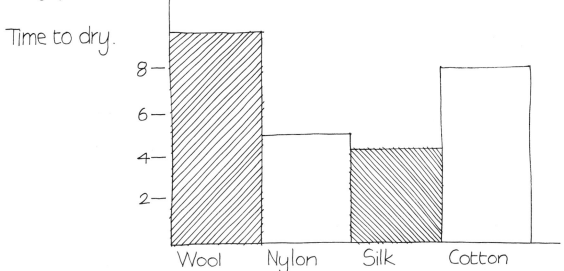

● Make a list and illustrate all the items that are washed with water at home and in school. The children could interview members of their families, their teachers and the school cleaners. The list might include: dishes, cars, bikes, windows, floors, clothing, tables, people, including hair and teeth, dogs, food, etc. The children could divide the items into two lists according to whether hot or cold water is used.

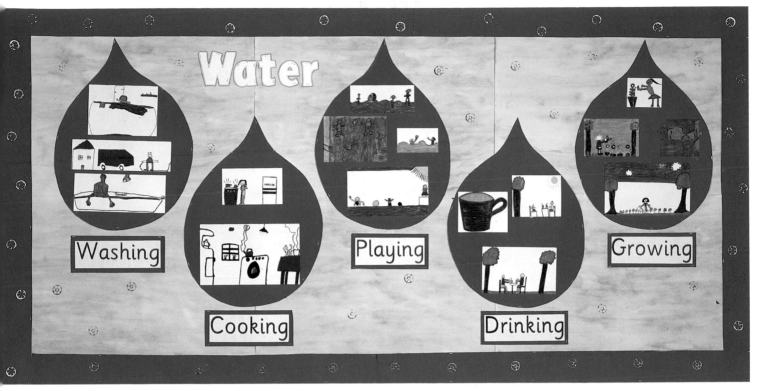

Raindrop display, see facing page

- List all the items of food that are cooked in water. The children could talk to the school cook about the water used to prepare food.
- Let the children experiment with soaking dried foods, for example, beans, lentils, peas, apricots, prunes, etc. The dried foods could be weighed before and after soaking, and the results compared.
- Make a collection of a variety of materials, for example, salt, soap powder, stone, metal, wood, plastic, sugar. Place each one in a container and ask the children to drip water on to the material. **The children could record their results in a graph or pictogram labelled:**
'Materials that are dissolved in water' and 'Materials that are not dissolved in water'.

- Make a collection of pictures of houses from different parts of the world. Ask the children to discuss what they can tell about the weather from looking at the house.

- If there is a freezer available in school, **make ice lollies with the children.** Have a selection of fruit juices for flavouring. Ice-making containers with a small stick placed in the liquid works well. Ask the children to make a mark in the container to show the level of the liquid. When the ice lollies have been frozen, and before they are eaten, ask the children to look carefully to see if they can still see the mark they made. Discuss with the children what has happened and what it means. Ask the children to describe the ice lolly: what it feels like, how it looks, if it has any smell, and compare it to how it looked, felt, smelt, before it was frozen.

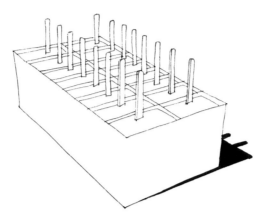

- **Ask the children to conduct a survey of the favourite drinks for the class.** Ask them to decide which ones involve adding water before drinking, for example, tea, fruit squash, etc., and which do not, for example lemonade, milk, fruit juice, etc.

- Get the children to draw the instructions for making a cup of tea, making sure they get the correct sequence.
- Plant some quick-growing seeds in a tray, for example, cress, bean sprouts. Ask them to water half the seeds and record the results. Sow further amounts of seeds and initially water all of them until they are growing well. Then stop watering half of the plants and record the results.
- Provide the children with some celery. **Put some water containing a food dye in a jar and leave the celery in the water for a few hours.** Ask the children to cut a section through the celery and discuss with them what they observe. Ask the children to draw what they see.

Cross section of celery.

- Ask individual children to prepare a brief talk for the rest of the class about any sport or activity they take part in that involves water, for example, swimming, fishing, keeping fish, canoeing, gardening, sailing model boats, helping to wash the car, etc.

This is a road drain. It takes the rain water away.

This is a manhole. It can be lifted up to look at the drain.

This is a fire hydrant. The firemen can find water here to help them put out a fire.

These pipes take dirty water away from the house. They come from the bath, the sink and the toilet.

WATER –
WHERE IT COMES FROM AND WHERE IT GOES

This is a reservoir. Water is collected and stored here.

These are water spouts on the church. They made special heads to decorate them.

This is the river. Water is taken from it and cleaned so it can go to the houses.

This is a water tower. Water is pumped to it and then it goes to the houses.

This is a village water pump. People used to come here to get all their water. It doesn't work anymore.

A WATER HUNT!

● Ask the children to walk around the school to look for all the places where there are taps. If possible, follow the pipes and discover what else is part of the system, for example, storage tank, central heating boiler, drains, toilets. Try to obtain architects' plans of the school and study them to discover where all the pipes go.

● Take the children to look at the outside of the school building. Ask them to look for all the things that might be connected with water, for example, gutters, drains, pipes, the shape of the roof, the roofing material, protection - if any - for windows, under window sills, overflow pipes, manhole covers.

● Take the children for a walk around the locality to look for further clues about water supply, collection or disposal. They may find the following: fire hydrant, water butt, drinking fountain, animal trough, outside tap, street gutter, manhole cover, high water mark from a flood, decorative fountain, sprinkler (in a garden), water tower, drain, etc.
If possible, take a camera and photograph any items connected with water. Mount a display of the photographs in the classroom and ask the children to help with the labelling. (See photograph above.)

● Ask the children to write to the Local Water Authority to ask for information about water collection, purifying, supply and disposal. It may be possible to organise a trip to the local sewage treatment works.

● Talk about the importance of a clean water supply. Investigate water projects in other countries.

PONDS, RIVERS AND SEAS

● Plan a visit to a local pond or lake.

Preparation
Make a collection of easy-to-use reference books that will help the children to identify the things they are likely to see. Familiarise the children with the books, and discuss with them what they think they might see.

Vocabulary
Ripples, cool, cold, still, deep, shallow, muddy, clear, clay, shingle, boggy, sandy, pebbles, rocks, bank, steep, living, growing, feeding, surface, margins, burrow, spawn, larvae, eggs, floating.

Form the children into small groups and equip each group with jars or transparent plastic containers, a magnifying glass, a net and drawing paper on a clipboard. An adult should work with each group to help them record and maybe identify the things the children find.

● In school, make a display of the children's paintings. As it is difficult to see some of the small animals or birds that may use a pond, encourage the children to use the reference books to add to the display. The teacher could make the background of the pond and the children could add drawings or paintings of their own. A pond picture could also be made in collage form (see photograph on facing page).

● Ask the children to make a very detailed drawing of a plant or piece of wood or stone, observing it through a magnifying glass.

● **Get the children to look up in a reference book the life cycle of a frog.** Ask them to draw the cycle.

● **Ask the children to find out about dragonflies** and their life cycle. Ask them to make a diagram of their findings.

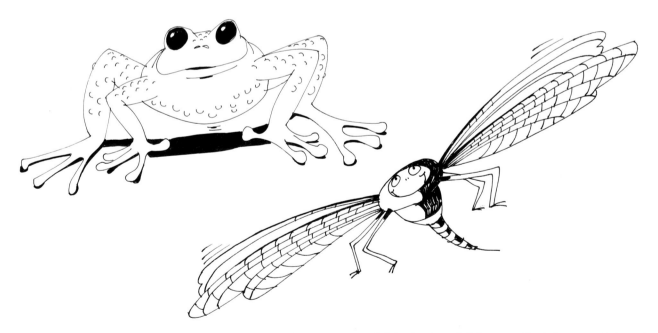

● Using a local Ordnance Survey map (1:25000 scale) help the children to find the pond they have visited. Look for other ponds, lakes, reservoirs and rivers in the area. Find the name of the nearest river. If possible, ask the children to find its source and where it goes. (A map of a wider area may be required for this.)

● Obtain some clay. Ask the children to weigh it and then let it dry out over a period of a few days. Weigh it again and ask the children to consider the results.

A pond collage, see facing page

SEAS AND OCEANS

- Use globes and maps to identify seas and oceans. Look at seas surrounding us. Name them.
- What food do we get from the sea? Ask the children to think about the fish they may see on sale, either fresh, frozen, smoked or tinned. If possible, visit a local supermarket and ask the children to list all the various forms of fish available. Ask the children to bring from home any packets or tins that once contained fish or fish products. Ask the children to look at the labels and discover the origins of the fish.
- Ask the children to use an atlas to find the places where fish have been caught. Display a map in the classroom and label the main sources of fish.
- Ask the children to draw (using a reference book) the most common fish that are caught for food.
- Make up a strong saline solution and ask the children to compare the taste with fresh water. Compare the buoyancy of fresh and salt water. A clay object is the best for this experiment.
- Ask the children about any journeys they have made across the sea. Trace the route in an atlas. Ask the children to list the seas or oceans they have crossed, or that members of their family have crossed.

Weather

● Introduce the topic by talking to the children about different kinds of weather. Ask the children to paint pictures of the different forms that they suggest. Collect reproductions of famous pictures which feature different weather forms to act as a stimulus for the children - for example, Van Gogh's 'The Sower' for sunshine, Bruegel's winter scenes for snow, Renoir's 'Umbrellas' for rain. Draw the children's attention to the way that the painters have represented the weather, using shadows in sunny scenes or the predominance of the colour grey in rainy scenes. Display the children's work.

A sunny picture.　　A foggy picture.　　A windy picture.

● Talk to the children about the present weather conditions. You may wish to create a chart where the children record the daily weather conditions over a given period of time. The degree of sophistication of data that the children collect will depend on their age and ability - for older children, provide them with a thermometer and a rain gauge to make quantitative recordings. At the end of the period ask the children to use the chart to summarise the weather, how many wet days, how many sunny days etc., or make bar charts of the daily temperatures or rainfall.

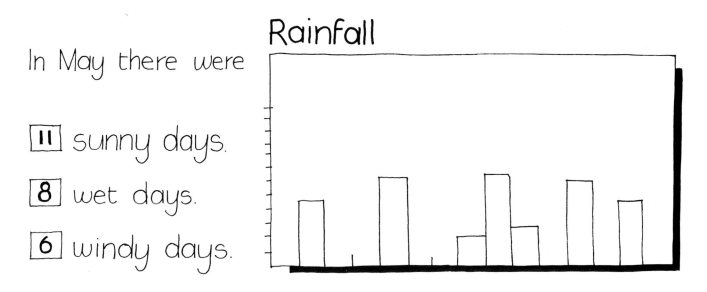

In May there were

[11] sunny days.

[8] wet days.

[6] windy days.

Rainfall

	Forecast	What happened
Monday	☀	☁
Tuesday	☁	☀
Wednesday	☀	☀
Thursday	FOG	☁
Friday	💧💧	💧💧

Weather forecasting

● Develop the idea of weather forecasting. Ask the children why they think that people want to know what the weather will be in the near future - the importance to farmers and sailors, and why ordinary people might be interested. Show the children examples of the symbols used in weather forecasting.

● Bring examples of newspaper weather forecasts for the children to look at and ask them to watch the forecasts on the television. Let them report to the class what the prediction was, and how accurate it was. The children use a chart to record the prediction and the actuality. (See photograph above.)

● Explain simply to the children how meteorologists use a variety of methods to forecast the weather. There are a number of information books which will support your explanation and provide pictures of weather satellites, etc.

● Talk about some of the folk lore methods that have been employed to predict the weather. These include things such as hanging up a piece of seaweed (if it was damp, rain was forecast), or traditional rhymes, for example 'Red sky at night, shepherds' delight. Red sky in the morning, shepherds' warning'. Investigate with the children how accurate these methods were. Let the children choose a method and forecast what the weather is likely to be. Ask them to record their forecast using appropriate symbols, and then see if it is accurate. Compare the accuracy of the various methods.

● Develop the idea of how the weather affects the children's lives. Discuss what they do in certain weather conditions. Make small books for the individual children. On each page, the children complete the sentence 'When it's.............. I ....', and illustrate their sentence.

● Talk about the different clothes that people wear in different weather. Cut out card shapes of people. Provide the children with different types of materials - thick cloth, thin cotton, plastic, etc. Ask the children to cut out clothes suitable for a particular type of weather, and to stick the clothes on the people shapes. Display the children's work with appropriate captions. (See photograph on facing page.)

Concentrate on different weather conditions.

WIND
● On a windy day, take the children into the playground. Tell them to stand still and to look around for a short time. When you return to the classroom, ask them what they felt. Record the words or phrases that they suggest. Question them on what they saw. You can prompt them by asking about trees in the vicinity, the movement of pieces of paper, smoke from chimneys, etc.

● Tell the children how the force of wind is described using the Beaufort scale and how it is determined through observation.

    0 - calm - smoke goes straight up
    1 - light air - smoke drifts
    2 - light breeze - leaves rustle, weather vanes move
    3 - gentle breeze - twigs move and flaps flap
    4 - moderate breeze - dust and paper blows in the street, small branches move
    5 - fresh breeze - small trees sway
    6 - strong breeze - large branches move
    7 - moderate gale - whole trees bend over
    8 - fresh gale - twigs break off
    9 - strong gale - chimneys and slates fall off
  10 - whole gale - trees uprooted, buildings damaged
  11 - storm - general destruction
  12 - hurricane - coasts flooded, devastation

With this information, record the force of wind each day.

Ask the children to illustrate the different forces of wind.

Force 0   Force 1   Force 2

● Talk about how the direction of the wind changes. Ask them to think of ways in which they could detect the wind direction - the sensation on their faces, the way trees are bending, from flags or pennants. On a windy day, take the children outside and see if they can tell from which direction the wind is coming.

● Discuss wind vanes with the children. If there are examples of wind vanes in the vicinity of the school take the children to see them, or find pictures of traditional designs. (For some children it may be appropriate to introduce the points of the compass with this work.) Ask the children to design wind vanes. Display by cutting out a large roof shape and sticking the children's vanes on top.

● Kites

Design kites with the children. Show them examples of different designs, the traditional diamond shaped kites, box kites and more intricate designs, particularly from other cultures, for example Chinese kites. The children design kites on paper and these are displayed in the classroom. Extend the activity by providing materials for the children to make their kites. Encourage the children to test their kites and modify them if necessary.

● Investigate other things that move in the wind.

● Paper Windmills

Show the children how to make model windmills. Cut out squares of paper (l5cm x 15cm). The children draw the diagonals using a ruler and then cut along the diagonals, stopping 3cm from the centre on each one. Ask the children to decorate their squares and then stick alternate corners to the middle. Make a small hole in the centre and attach it to a stick. (Impress on the children the need to be very careful with the sticks.) Put the windmills in flower pots and place them outside to see how they move.

● Tell the children how windmills were used in the past to grind corn and how they are now used in 'windfarms' to generate electricity.

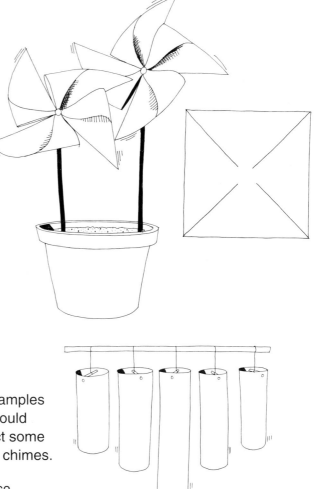

● Wind Chimes

Talk about wind chimes. If possible, bring in examples to show the children. Discuss what materials would be suitable to use to make wind chimes. Collect some of the materials and allow the children to make chimes.

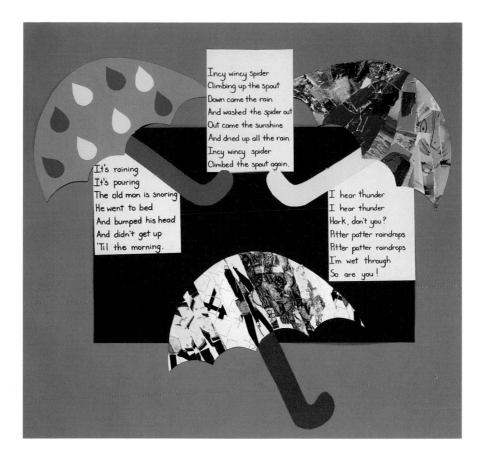

The following rhymes appear on the umbrella display:

Incy wincy spider
Climbing up the spout
Down came the rain
And washed the spider out
Out came the sunshine
And dried up all the rain
Incy wincy spider
Climbed the spout again.

It's raining
It's pouring
The old man is snoring
He went to bed
And bumped his head
And didn't get up
'Til the morning.

I hear thunder
I hear thunder
Hark, don't you?
Pitter patter raindrops
Pitter patter raindrops
I'm wet through
So are you!

RAIN

- Discuss with the children why rain is so necessary. Ask them to make a list of all the reasons that they can think of. (This work has clear links with the Water topic.) Tell them about countries that have extremes of rainfall, desert or drought-affected areas, and lands that have monsoons or flooding. Highlight any news items that relate to rainfall.
- Talk about what people wear when it is raining, and the type of waterproof materials that are used to make the clothing. Provide the children with a range of materials and ask them to discover which would be suitable for making a waterproof garment. The children record how they made their discoveries.
- A colourful display can be made by asking the children to design umbrellas. Cut out umbrella shapes which the children then paint. Encourage them to use rain motifs in their designs.
- Teach the children rhymes and poems that have a rain theme, for example, 'Doctor Foster', 'Rain, rain, go away', and 'It's raining, it's pouring'. Children write out the poems and decorate their writing. Display these around the umbrella designs. (See photograph above.)

SUN

- Talk to the children about the solar system, and how the earth is just one of the planets that move around the sun. Give the children some basic information about the sun. Let a small group of children paint a large sun. Provide them with bright thick paints for the task. Write out the 'Sun facts' and stick them on the sun.
- Talk about why the sun is so important to life. List the ideas generated by the children. Ask the children to explain why they can see the sun on some days and not on others.

The sun is a ball of gas.

Seasons

Discussion

Rehearse with the children the cycle of the seasons. Talk about different weather conditions associated with each season of the year. Talk about the activities that children like to do at different times of the year.

● Hold a brainstorming session in which children contribute their favourite activities associated with each season. Make a large mapping chart for each season.

walking in the park

looking at the pond

eating Easter eggs

SPRING

looking at baby animals

flying my kite

planting seeds

● Ask children to choose their favourite season of the year and to say why. Make a graph to show which is the most popular time of the year.
● Go for a 'Signs of Spring' walk. Choose a typical spring day and take groups of children along a chosen route. Listen and look for the sights, sounds and smells of spring. Ask the children to draw a map of the route taken, recording their observations and where they discovered things.
● Investigate festivals that occur in each season and look at the symbols associated with them. How appropriate are they to each season?
● From ancient times people have looked forward to the coming of spring after the long, cold, dark days of winter. Early winter festivals celebrated the fact that the shortest day of winter was over. Songs and poems were written to celebrate Maytime.
● Spring was often depicted as a person (a young girl) by artists and poets. Eggs were given as a spring gift even in pre-Christian times, as they symbolise new life. Find out about Easter games to play: egg rolling, egg tossing, egg and spoon races, egg hunting, decorating eggs, and making Easter bonnets.
● Autumn celebrations include harvest festivals, the gathering of fruits and giving thanks, and preparations for the hard winter months ahead. Churches are decorated with displays of special loaves, flowers, fruit and vegetables.
● Winter is traditionally seen as a time of rest. Some creatures hibernate, and many trees are dormant, waiting for warmer temperatures. Evergreen plants are signs of life in the darkness of winter.
● Find out about seasonal festivals belonging to world faiths, e.g. Holi, the Indian spring festival. Read 'The Wicked King and his Good Son' in Madhur Jaffrey's *Seasons of Splendour,* Pavilion Books.
● Build up a library of photographs of the school grounds at different times of the year.

Tracing paper used to make seasonal picture window display

● Focus upon one or two deciduous trees in the school grounds or in the local area, and chart seasonal changes with the children by taking photographs, collecting leaves and fruits, by sketching and recording observations in a 'tree diary'.

● Look at how the seasons are depicted in the works of famous artists. Fine art calendars and greetings cards are a good source of pictures.

● Read *The Selfish Giant* by Oscar Wilde. Paint 'before and after' pictures of the giant's garden, or **make two mobiles, one depicting the winter garden with the lonely giant, and the other showing the spring garden with the children.**

● Collect poems and make an illustrated anthology of seasonal poems. Each group of poems can be mounted on different coloured paper.

● Ask the children to write acrostic poems based on the words AUTUMN, WINTER, SPRING and SUMMER.

> **A**utumn is the time for crunching leaves
> **U**nder my feet,
> **T**aking walks in the park and picking
> **U**p conkers,
> **M**aking bonfires and eating
> **N**uts.

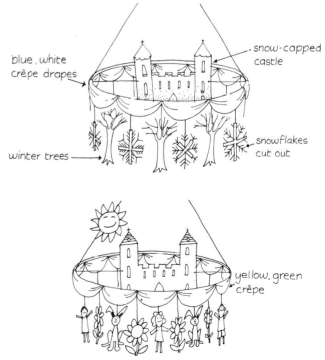

blue, white crêpe drapes

snow-capped castle

winter trees

snowflakes cut out

yellow, green crêpe

Ideas for large classroom displays

● Tie strings across the classroom from corner to corner. Decorate each quarter of the room with seasonal colours and hang streamers and topical mobiles from each section of the string.

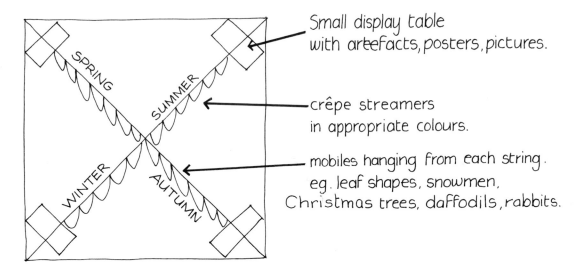

Small display table with artefacts, posters, pictures.

crêpe streamers in appropriate colours.

mobiles hanging from each string. eg. leaf shapes, snowmen, Christmas trees, daffodils, rabbits.

● **Make a 'four seasons' display on a long table.** Divide the table into four sections, and cover each section with an appropriate colour. Collect objects and pictures associated with the different seasons, and display them in the appropriate section. (See drawing.)

green, yellow, orange, blue and white paper in bands.

Seasonal picture displayed in cut-out window.

turn

decorate with pictures cut from seed catalogues.

● **Make season wheels as** shown in the line drawing.

● Make a window display. Paint and stick tissue paper onto large sheets of tracing paper to make pictures of typical seasonal views. (See photograph on page 65.)

● Discuss 'unseasonal weather', and the degree of variation from year to year. Talk about the effect upon farmers, etc. Ask the children whether it always snows in winter in this part of the country. Are our summers always hot? Compare seasonal weather conditions in different areas of the country. Perhaps, when carrying out a comparison of the home region with another locality, penfriends could exchange weather bulletins covering the same period of time.

● Research seasonal changes in other parts of the world. Invite people into school who have first-hand experience of living in different climatic regions. Find out about the monsoon season, wet and dry seasons.

● Investigate the life cycles of creatures and plants in relation to seasonal changes. Find out about hibernating animals.

● Explain, with the aid of a large diagram, how seasons occur.

● Find out about the summer solstice, winter solstice, the vernal or spring equinox, autumn equinox, the northern hemisphere and the southern hemisphere.

Comparison of the home area with another locality

● When choosing a locality to compare with your home area, it is important to choose one that will provide sufficient differences for the children to examine. The work is enhanced if you can arrange a visit to the area, and therefore it is advantageous if the area of comparison is not too far away. Certain factors may influence your choice: for example, you may have existing contacts with another school in a different area. Consider the local area: is it predominantly rural or urban?; is it close to the sea?; what are the primary industries?

Once you have decided on the area that you are going to use for comparison, inform the children. Show them where the town is on a map - make sure that the children can show you where their home town or village is located to enable them to compare the locations. Encourage the children to deduce features about the other area from the map.

● Tell the children that you want to find out as much about the other area as possible, and ask them to think of ways that they could gather the information. (You may find that the children have visited the area or have family or friends living there.) If the children have difficulty thinking of ideas, you can suggest some: writing to local organisations, for example, tourist offices, town halls, council etc. Talk to the children about how to write formal letters requesting information. The children then write the letters. If the children are sent information, show this to the whole class. Allow them to deduce as much from this information as possible.

● One of the most profitable ways of discovering information is to establish links with a school in your chosen area and to develop a system of penfriends. This requires close liaison with the teachers in the other school. When the children write to their penfriends they will probably wish to tell their friends about themselves, but impress on the children that they are also endeavouring to seek information about the other area. Discuss the possible questions that they may wish to ask.

● You can use other media to establish links between the two schools. The children can send taped messages, photographs, and videos that the classes have made. Schools can also, now, communicate by computer networks. These media provide a wealth of information and can reveal surprising facts about other areas - tapes may show that the local dialect is different from the children's own speech.

As you build up the data, make a large classroom display about the comparison area. Include any published materials that the children have acquired, penfriend letters, photographs, etc.

Our penfriends live in Truro

Truro is by the sea

Use the display to synthesise the information discovered by the children. Make out a grid of 'basic facts' about the area. These include size of settlement, main occupations, main recreations, transport available, number of schools, churches, temples, etc.

Truro

Population	20.000
Number of schools	8
Number of cathedrals	1

- If you are able to visit the area, involve the children in planning the trip. One of the highlights will, obviously, be meeting the penfriends, but use the opportunity to visit as much of the area as possible. Suggest that the children ask their penfriends' advice about the features of the area that are particularly worthy of a visit. Plan the day so that the children have the chance to record features of the area by sketching. Add these drawings to your main display. The children can write to thank all those who helped them arrange the trip and those who provided hospitality.

- Plan a reciprocal visit from the penfriends. Involve the children, again, in the planning. Ask them what they think their friends would like to see, and any features that could be regarded as 'typical' of your area. Work out a schedule for the day. Ensure when planning the day that there are times when the visitors can relax, eat, etc. Talk with the children about how long the journey will take and the transport that the visitors will use. Take photographs to record the visit.

- To conclude this work, brainstorm with the children all the similarities and differences that they found between the two areas. Write down the children's ideas on large pieces of paper. Ask the children to draw pictures to illustrate the similarities and differences that they have identified. Display the papers with the children's drawings around them.

Comparison of the home area with a locality overseas

Any comparison of life in a contrasting locality overseas should, whenever possible, be approached through direct contact with people living in that environment. Contact can be made by establishing penfriend links, through personal contacts made by teachers and schools.

If this is not possible, educational materials produced by ActionAid and OXFAM can provide teachers with the detailed information and personal accounts of everyday life that are essential for meaningful, in-depth study of an area overseas. Catalogues of these educational materials are available from ActionAid and OXFAM (addresses are given on page 72).

Teachers will need to acquire considerable background information relating to one small area - a town or village - of a similar size to the home locality. Resources needed will include photographs showing buildings and landscape, maps and plans, details of the weather, transport, diet, clothes, housing, employment, education, leisure pursuits, festivals and special occasions, and descriptions of recent changes that have taken place in the area.

- In the initial teaching session, find out what the children already know about the place to be studied. Stress the fact that the town or village that you will be looking at is just one part of the country. Discuss the differences that can be found within most countries, including our own, and compile a list: urban or rural, coastal or inland settlement, wealth and poverty, high or low land, different climatic and weather conditions, different religious beliefs, and languages spoken. Refer to the information gathered during studies of the local area and comparisons made with another locality within the UK.
- Locate the area to be studied on a world map or globe. Name the continent, bordering countries, oceans or seas, mountain ranges, towns and cities. Look at the position of the country in relation to the UK. Prepare a fact file about Peru, for example, listing the main areas and geographical features of the country, and locating its position within South America. Indicate where the town or village to be studied is located within Peru.
- Collect artefacts from the country being studied: postcards, posters, photographs, travel guides, brochures, souvenirs, musical instruments, story books, clothing and fabrics, coins, stamps, flags and produce. Display artefacts with maps and fact file as shown in the photograph.
- Plan an imaginary journey to the chosen country. Plan the route, mode of transport, etc., using the travel brochures and atlas. What would you take with you? What currency would you need?
- Obtain details about family life. Exchange photographs and personal accounts with penfriends. Make your own 'family tree' to send to your penfriend, and compare with details of a Peruvian family.
- Write your own account of 'A day in the life of......' and compare it with that of your penfriend. Include times of the day such as times of getting up and going to bed. Make a zigzag book to illustrate the 24 hour time-line.
- Investigate the work carried out by adults, and find out how they earn a living. What kinds of skills are needed? Look at the contribution made by the children in the household, and compare with the jobs that you do to help your family.
- Exchange photographs of teachers, children and school buildings. Include photographs of children engaged in typical school activities, and add a commentary describing what is happening in the picture. Follow the route that the Peruvian children take to school on a large-scale map and compare it with your own journey.
- Find out about leisure activities enjoyed by the children. Exchange details of interests, sports, collections, and hobbies. Ask your exchange partners what games they enjoy playing - are some of them similar to the games you play?
- Find out about dwellings. If possible, gather information about materials used, the dimensions and facilities of an actual home. Try to obtain photographs of the inside of homes. Ask the children to draw plans of their own homes to make a comparison.
- Investigate shopping and marketing. Find out how people travel to the shops or market, and what they buy and sell. Compare shopping lists.
- Make a study of how the landscape affects people's ability to move around. Try to find out details of distances to be travelled and the terrain to be crossed to reach the nearest market, school, or to travel to work.
- Find out how the weather and climate of the area affects the way people live, the crops that they grow, the animals they keep, their health, and the clothes they wear.
- Use large-scale maps of the area to practise map skills such as identifying main features, using grid references, calculating distances and finding directions.

The Thunder King
A folk tale from Peru

The condor flew to the top of the mountain.

He helped Illanti to rescue his brother from the ice palace.

Paint and collage pictures based on The Thunder King story

Find out about the history of the country being studied, the languages spoken, and how and why people have settled where they have. Look at any recent changes to the environment, and perhaps debate the possible advantages and disadvantages of economic development.

Investigate festivals and customs and find out how special occasions are celebrated.

Listen to folk music from the region and find out about the traditional musical instruments.

Exchange tapes of modern popular music with your contact school.

Myths, legends and folk tales convey a tremendous 'sense of place', and often include animals and geographical features of a locality. Legends can sometimes offer folklore explanations for natural phenomena. Illustrate stories using paint and collage materials. See photograph above of 'The Thunder King' display. (*The Thunder King,* by Amanda Loverseed, Blackie,).

Exchange recipes of favourite meals. Cook using ingredients from the country you are studying. Use any local expertise available, for example, contact restaurants and ask for information.

Look at things you can buy in this country from your overseas area. Find out if things from this country can be bought in your chosen country.

Make a collection of unusual artefacts (or pictures of them) and ask children to guess what they are and what they are used for.

Write letters to various agencies, for example tourist boards, travel companies, food manufacturers, asking for additional information.

● Use traditional arts and crafts and images of the area being studied to inspire creative activities. (See photograph on page 2 of 'batik' pictures inspired by St. Lucia.)

Batik pictures (see photograph on page 2): Crayon a simple but colourful design, pressing heavily so that there is a thick layer of wax over the whole piece of paper. Screw the picture into a tight ball, cracking the surface of the wax layer. Flatten the picture and apply a wash of drawing ink of a contrasting colour. Place a blank piece of paper over the picture and iron immediately.

Educational materials catalogue available from:
- OXFAM, Campaigns/Development Education Team, 274 Banbury Road, Oxford, OX2 7DZ, England. (Telephone 0865.313176)
- ActionAid, Hamlyn House, Archway, London N19 5PG, England. (Telephone 071.281-4101).

Book References
Rosie's Walk, Pat Hutchins (Picture Puffin)
Bears in the Night, S. and J. Berenstain (Collins)
We're Going on a Bear Hunt, Michael Rosen (Walker Books)

For details of further Belair Publications please write to:
BELAIR PUBLICATIONS LTD
P.O. Box 12, Twickenham, TW1 2QL
England

For sales and distribution (outside USA and Canada):
FOLENS PUBLISHERS,
Albert House, Apex Business Centre,
Boscombe Road, Dunstable, Bedfordshire, LU5 4RL,
England

For sales and distribution in North America:
INCENTIVE PUBLICATIONS INC.
3835 Cleghorn Avenue, Nashville, Tn 372l5, U.S.A.

Books in the Belair series

LANGUAGE
Language in Colour
Words with Wings
Rainbow Year
On First Reading
Sounds Like This
Paint a Poem

MATHS
Maths on Display
The Maths Collection

SCIENCE
The Art of Science

CROSS-CURRICULAR
Display for all Seasons
A World of Display
Themes Familiar
Classwise
Tales for Topics
In a Moment
Storytime Topics

ART AND CRAFT
Simply Artistic
Something Special
Handwork Skills and Themes
A Work of Art
Material Pleasures

HUMANITIES
Starting with Me
A Sense of Place
Picture the Past

MUSIC, DANCE AND DRAMA
Music Works
Just Imagine
Time to Dance (book)
Time to Dance (cassette)
Of Frogs and Snails

FOOD AND COOKERY
The Spice of Life

BEHAVIOUR
A Positive Approach

INTERACTIVE DISPLAY
Hands on Display

THE ABC COLLECTION
ABC Big Book
ABC Poster Book
ABC Children's Book (hardback)
ABC Children's Book (paperback)
ABC Teacher Resource Book

THE LITTLE BELL series
Paper Capers
Hats in a Hurry
With Best Wishes
Present Times
Let's Make a Book
Creative Christmas
Making and Baking

A Sense of Place presents activities which develop geographical skills through the study of places and themes, for children from five to nine years.

ISBN 0 947882 53 7

ISBN 0-947882-53-7

9 780947 882532 >

Belair Publications Ltd